the BANNER book

the BANNER book

RUTH ANN LOWERY

Chilton Book Company

Radnor, Pennsylvania

On the half title page: *Plant a juicy slice of watermelon in your garden with this cheery banner. Or, why not use a banner like this one at a school or church picnic? Visitors would certainly be able to tell where they could pick up a tasty slice of watermelon to fill their plates. This banner was designed and sewn by Michele Shepler.*

Designed by Anthony Jacobson
Manufactured in the United States of America

A Cataloging in Publication record for this book is available from the Library of Congress

2 3 4 5 6 7 8 9 0   4 3 2 1 0 9 8 7 6 5

To my father,

Robert Thomas,

and in memory of my mother,

Ruth Haughton Thomas,

for teaching us that we could accomplish
anything that we "set our minds to."

A special thank you to my husband,

Keith,

and daughters,

Amy and Sally,

for always supporting me in anything
that I "set my mind to."

Contents

Foreword
by Sue Hausmann

Banners! What fun! They symbolize a celebration. Each one says something different. What a special way to share our joys!

When I first met Ruth Ann Lowery several years ago, she came into my classroom to assist. What a treat to have Ruth Ann to help the students with any questions from technique to technical.

When Ruth Ann began to design her wonderful banners, she quickly created patterns for seasonal, special interest, and special occasion decorating. The beautiful and durable all-weather banners waving in the Pittsburgh wind caused numerous people to stop in to ask Ruth Ann how long the store had been there and how they could buy a banner. Ruth Ann replied, "For years. Would you like to learn how to make a banner for your home?" And many did. While teaching hundreds of banner classes, Ruth Ann has perfected the patterns and techniques for you to enjoy in this *Banner Book*.

We have enjoyed having Ruth Ann as a guest on our "Art of Sewing with Sue Hausmann" public television series, on programs #208 and #709, sharing several types of banners. Her techniques for reversible appliqué are quick, easy and sturdy.

Whether you plan to create a flag for your front porch, a liturgical banner for your church or a stained-glass-window banner for your apartment, *The Banner Book* will give you step-by-step instruction and encouragement. Be prepared to celebrate your special joys with Ruth Ann's special banners!

Preface

I can still remember how proud I was of my first sewing project, a brown A-line skirt. When I was the first one to finish in my seventh-grade home economics class, I couldn't wait to start my next project. After all, now I was an expert! So, of course, I selected a dress pattern with a front and back yoke plus set-in sleeves. That was a humbling experience.

My mother sewed, but she never used a pattern for clothing or home decorating projects. She said, "Reading all of those instructions gets on my nerves!" The only patterns I can remember her using were the templates for appliquéd quilts. When I needed help with a pattern I had purchased, I asked my Dad. He was a machinist and could read any kind of blueprint. It was my Dad who got me through those yokes and set-in sleeves.

After high school I attended Penn State for mechanical engineering technology, got married, and had two children. I started an electrician apprenticeship, attended Point Park College for electrical engineering technology, and became a journeyman electrician. I have been employed as an electrician, electronic repair person, electrical engineer, automation engineer, and a process control engineer. But I never quit sewing.

In 1991, I decided that working in the steel industry was not what I wanted to do with the rest of my life. I became the manager of one of the locations of Gloria Horn Sewing Studios in Pittsburgh, Pennsylvania.

Since 1988, I had been making performance props and flags of all types for our high school band. When decorative outdoor banners started to appear on homes and businesses, I was immediately interested. We started to teach the reversible appliqué technique at our shop in May 1992. The response was incredible!

By fall of 1992, Gloria Horn and I had finished our first book, *A Banner Year*. It has instructions and patterns for reversible outdoor banners. We fol-

The Bluebird of Happiness will certainly visit if you hang this beautiful, stained-glass-window style banner. Because of the reversible appliqué technique used to make it, light can shine through the single layer of nylon fabric, causing the colors to literally glow. This banner was designed and sewn by Michele Shepler.

lowed with a complete line of banner, garden flag, and stained-glass-window patterns and supplies.

We have received a flood of requests for indoor banner ideas, so I have included both indoor and outdoor designs in this book. Special thanks for many of the designs go to my dear friend and coworker, Michele Shepler. She is not only a talented designer, she also made many of the beautiful banners featured. I'm sure you'll find everything you need to know to complete a banner in this book. You can try my projects or create designs of your own.

A banner is a wonderful gift to a friend or relative. They can also be contributions to such worthy causes as churches, food banks, or the United Way. Let your creative juices flow and have fun.

Introduction:
Why Banners?

When you think about the word banner, what picture comes to mind? I immediately see a street in a small town with a long, narrow sign hanging over Main Street. It might announce the town's Bicentennial, Founder's Day, Firemen's Fair, or any other celebration that residents anticipate. The next vision that comes to mind is of the banners that hang in our local school. They proudly display the school name and mascot. Sometimes they include information about championships won or records that were broken. Another banner that some of us see weekly is the one hanging in our place of worship. It can proclaim any number of reasons to rejoice. Religious banners sometimes are opulent, made with satins or lamés and ornamented with beads. The most common are the banners made by Sunday school classes, which are usually made from felt and glue. Most recently, the term banner refers to the decorative flags hanging outside homes and businesses all over the country.

I think the reason banners of all types are so popular was best described by my dear friend Margie Evans. She said that everyone likes banners because they make us smile. A celebration in our town . . . a championship football, basketball, or track team . . . a religious holiday . . . a party, a birth, a graduation or a wedding . . . these are things that make us smile. Now you will see how easy it is to create your own smiles with the projects and instructions included in this book. I hope you enjoy learning all the different banner techniques I have included. Try to learn something new every day and keep the spirit of sewing alive!

Remember that banners of all types are usually viewed from a distance. Little mistakes are not visible. So try to put perfection aside for awhile. Sit back, relax, select a project, and smile.

Chapter 1

Materials, Supplies, and Hardware

Reversible appliqué banners glow with color when the light shines through them. Although usually used outdoors, stained-glass-window style banners like this one make great window decorations: They provide beautiful color indoors in the daytime. At night, when they're illuminated from within, they shine for passers-by to admire.

Banners can be made from almost any material. The fabric, thread, and other supplies you use for each project depend on the project itself. Where the banner will be used, how it will be viewed, and what construction technique you want to use all affect the best materials for the project.

In this chapter, I will introduce you to what I think are the best supplies and notions for making the various types of banners and fabrics. You'll find complete details on the techniques used to create banners in Chapter 2, Banner-Making Techniques, and Chapter 3, Appliqué.

Please experiment with ideas of your own. Make small samples, using something you are just dying to try. Then do some research and development on your sample. Put it out in the weather, throw it in the washing machine, have it dry-cleaned, expose the sample to the same conditions the finished banner will face. The extra time it takes to make a sample will pay off in the long run: Losing a sample is much easier than losing an entire project.

Selecting Fabrics and Threads

Certain fabrics are ideal for outdoors banners, which generally need to be reversible so they can be seen from both sides. Other more formal and luxurious fabrics, like satins and lamés, are definitely limited to indoor use. If you want to use no-sew techniques, choose materials of solid construction (non woven), such as felt or Ultrasuede.

Fabrics for Indoor Banners

Indoor banners can be made from almost any fabric. The theme can determine the fabric, but before you make your selection, decide if the final product will need to be cleaned often. This may determine whether you go with washable or dry-cleanable fabrics. If you are making the first banner in a series, make it from a fabric that will be readily available to others at a later date. If you need to make a large number of a particular design, use a no-sew technique.

Formal indoor banners, such as those with religious motifs or works of art, are usually viewed up close and for an extended period of time. For this reason, you'll want to pay extra attention to details: You want to create a banner that is interesting and worthy of the viewer's attention. Fabrics like satin, lamé, moiré, velvet, linen, silk, and Ultrasuede are excellent for creating a dramatic effect on formal indoor banners. You can also find beautiful 100 percent cotton fabric with metallic gold accents that are easy to work with. (The Angel Banner project in Chapter 6 is a formal project that features many of these fabrics.)

Of course, embellishments in the form of metallic threads, beads, decorative machine stitching, thread painting, and appliqué, to name a

Indoor banners like this felt design that was cut and glued, make excellent projects for children. The Sunday school classes of Prince of Peace Lutheran Church, Pittsburgh, Pennsylvania, make these banners to be displayed in church during the various seasons of the year.

few, can turn the most ordinary materials into something extraordinary. Before you add them, though, make sure the base or background fabrics you have chosen are sturdy enough to support the embellishment technique without sagging. If you choose a soft or limp base fabric because of other qualities that it possesses, you may need to add extra stabilization to it in the form of interfacing, batting, or fleece. If you choose to add batting or fleece, you will need to sew through all of the layers by quilting or tying. Quilting and tying can be done by hand or machine.

Another type of indoor banner is the athletic or school activities banner. These usually hang high in a gymnasium or behind the glass in a lobby trophy case. They will probably never be laundered and seldom dry-cleaned, if at all. Felt is a good, inexpensive choice for banners of this type. Use a high-quality felt that will hold its shape whether you appliqué, fuse, or glue your design. Wool felt is, of course, the best quality, but it is expensive and not always readily available. Polyester felts sold by the yard work very well, and are washable. Don't purchase acrylic felts usually sold in small squares as "Craft Felt." The felt pulls apart and shreds too easily; acrylics are also known for pilling and balling with wear.

Fabrics for Outdoor Banners

You'll need to use a different set of criteria to select fabric for outdoor banners. Will the banner keep its color for a reasonable amount of time, even in the summer's sun? Will the fabric dry quickly after a rainstorm, thus resisting mold and mildew? Will the fabric be lightweight enough to have a nice transparent quality? Any fabric that can hold up outdoors will be washable.

Outdoor banners require different construction techniques, too, because they will be subjected to various weather conditions. They will need to be appliquéd, rather than fused or glued.

For outdoor banners or garden flags of any type, I recommend using 200 denier (pronounced duh-NEER) nylon fabric, which is available in a myriad of colors. Be sure to only purchase nylon that has a UV protective coating. This coating resists fading and rotting due to the sun: Sunlight will destroy untreated nylon in a matter of months. The nylon fabric is lightweight and transparent, yet strong and durable. It dries quickly after a rainstorm, which reduces the risk of mold and mildew. Nylon is also machine-washable and easy to work with.

Because outdoor banners are usually viewed from a distance while moving in a vehicle, they need to be understood and appreciated in a short period of time. The transparent quality of 200 denier nylon, along with the reversible appliqué technique you'll read about in Chapter 3, yields a banner that is bright and identifiable. Banners sewn from heavier fabrics, or with construction techniques that result in multiple layers of fabric, are dark and heavy and thus not as effective. If you can't find 200 denier nylon in your area, encourage your local fabric/sewing stores to carry it. Or look for a mail-order source. See "Sources of Supplies" at the end of this book for companies that sell banner fabrics and banner-making supplies.

A word of caution: Don't try to appliqué with ripstop nylon. Although it has many wonderful uses, banner making isn't one of them. Trying to appliqué with ripstop nylon could cause you to swear off banners forever.

Threads for Banner Making

The most important ingredient in a banner, next to the fabric, is the thread. The main thing to consider is quality. The finished project is only as good as the materials used in it.

Indoor banners can be sewn with any type of thread. Metallics, lamés (such as Sulky Sliver and Horn of America's Stream lamé), rayons, acrylics, cottons, and polyesters, as well as invisible thread, are all suitable for indoor use. Remember to match the style of thread to the fabrics used in the banner. Elegant fabrics like satin, lamé, velvet, and moiré cry out for decorative threads. Combining them with metallic, lamé, rayon, or acrylic thread will create a luxurious, opulent effect. Bear in mind that the method of cleaning may be a consideration when selecting thread. Remember to check the manufacturer's recommendations. You can read more about using different threads and fabrics in the Angel Banner project in Chapter 6.

Let the pattern and fabric dictate the type of thread you choose. For example, an indoor banner created of 100 percent cotton fabric might be appliquéd with cotton or polyester thread. Banners made with invisible appliqué require invisible thread. The Strawberry Banner in Chapter 5 uses monofilament .004 mm nylon for the invisible appliqué.

Outdoor reversible banners are assembled with fusible thread. It has a polyester core covered with a heat-activated coating that allows the thread to become a fusing agent. Fusible thread is easy to identify: It looks like dental floss. Think of it as Heat 'n' Bond or Wonder-Under in thread form. With it you can fuse the edges of a design, yet still trim the back side away later. Fusible thread is the heart of the reversible appliqué technique I use. (See "Reversible Appliqué" on page 39 for directions.)

Fusible thread also can come in handy with appliqué patterns that are not intended to be reversible, because you can use it to anchor the pieces by sewing around the edges only. This will give the finished design a softer appearance than the stiff, ironed-down look of pieces that have been entirely fused. There are two fusible threads on the market that I am aware of: Thread Fuse and Stitch 'n' Fuse.

Fusibles and Stabilizers for Fabric

Fusibles

Paper-backed fusible web products, such as Heat 'n' Bond and Wonder-Under, are fusing agents for creating appliquéd projects of any type. They hold the design in place and keep the edges of the fabric from fraying. The fusing agent is a heat-activated web that is sprayed onto a paper backing. When you place the web side onto the wrong side of your fabric, and warm the paper side with your iron, the web fuses to your fabric. Always follow manufacturer's instructions when using fusible products.

To cut out your design, peel the paper from the back of your design piece and iron it onto your base fabric. You'll find more detailed directions on using fusibles in the instructions for individual projects as well as on page 26, "Using Fusibles for Appliqué."

When choosing a fusing agent, be sure to select a sewable type. All manufacturers of fusible products make different weights of their fusing agents, and some are meant to be fused only, not sewn. If you try to sew through a fusing agent not designed for that purpose, you will gum up your needle and keep breaking threads. Also choose a fusible that is as lightweight as possible: Heavy-weight fusibles on light-weight fabrics make appliqué look and feel stiff.

Stabilizers

Most fabrics require extra stabilization when you are doing appliqué or decorative stitching. There are many types of stabilizers to choose from. The fabric and technique will determine the type of stabilizer you'll need.

Tearaway, the oldest and most well-known stabilizer, is a heavy paper with a rough texture that resembles non-woven interfacing. To use it, you simply place it under your fabric, next to the feed dogs of your sewing machine, sew it in place as you appliqué, then tear it off when you are done. Generally, you don't even need to pin it in place. Tearaway works great on dense satin-stitched appliqué or heavily stitched decorative stitches. Delicate stitching can become distorted when the heavy tearaway is removed.

Iron-on tearaway has a waxed side that fuses temporarily to fabric when warmed lightly with an iron. It is a good stabilizer for slippery fabrics like the nylon used for outdoor banners. While other stabilizers can shift and bunch in the sewing machine as they slide against the fabric, the temporary wax fusing on iron-on tearaway eliminates this problem. In addition, iron-on stabilizers are softer and more pliable that the standard tearaways. This is especially helpful when making large appliqué banners, because you need something that is easy to roll or bunch up to fit through the body of the sewing machine.

Liquid stabilizers are poured or painted onto fabric, and are either left to dry overnight or are blown dry with a hair dryer. Fabric treated with these products becomes extremely stiff and able to support decorative stitches without pinching up or tunneling. Liquid stabilizers have an important advantage: After you have finished sewing your project, laundering removes them completely from the fabric. The tearaways leave a small amount of paper behind. Of course, you wouldn't use this type of stabilizer on a non-washable fabric.

Spray-on liquid stabilizers are easier and neater to use than the ones that are poured or painted onto the fabric. You can apply them exactly where you need them, and there is also less waste. The best way to use them is to apply a light coat and allow it to air-dry or blow it dry with a hair dryer. Once it is dry, spray on another coat if you need more stiffness. This product also needs to be laundered away and shouldn't be used on non-washable fabrics.

Heat-removed stabilizers are the latest to hit the market and are the best choice for non-washable fabrics. They look like a piece of fine needlepoint canvas and are simply removed with a warm iron after you've finished doing your appliqué or decorative stitching. When warmed with an iron, the stabilizer turns dark brown and flakes cleanly off the fabric, leaving no residue that needs to be laundered out. Because they don't need to be torn off the fabric, there's no danger of stitching becoming distorted.

Marking, Measuring, and Using Patterns

Marking Tools

Marking tools are used in every type of banner. When possible I use a felt-tip, wash-away marker to trace appliqué designs. On non-washable fabrics I suggest using a felt-tip, disappearing marker. Just be aware that if you have to put your project aside for a while, the disappearing ink may be gone when you are able to pick it up again. For nylon fabrics, chalk pencils seem to be the best markers because felt tip ones simply "puddle up" on the nylon. Whatever style of marker you choose, be sure that your marks will not show on your finished banner. Test all markers on a scrap of your banner fabric. You need to make sure they will be visible while you are sewing, and easy to remove when you are finished.

Tracing Tables

Tracing tables make any tracing chore much easier. I think it is important to have a table that is lightweight, portable, inexpensive, and unbreakable. There are a variety of homemade setups you can use for tracing, including putting a lamp under a glass-top table or placing a sheet of glass over a cardboard box with a light bulb in it. In a pinch, you can always trace on a window. All have their drawbacks. Lamps and incandescent light bulbs get hot and become uncomfortable to work around if you are tracing an intricate design. A sheet of glass or glass-top table does not diffuse the light, causing glaring that is hard on the eyes. Tracing on a window is very tiresome if you are working on a big design, and is an option only in the daytime.

Are we proud of our pets? You bet we are. They're also a great source of inspiration for banner patterns. This Persian cat was sewn by author Ruth Ann Lowery and given as a gift to her in-laws, Lillian and Bud Lowery. Now everyone on their street knows that Comet is the real boss in their house!

The best tracing table I have seen is the Quilters Portable Tracing Table available from Me-Sew Inc. They come in three sizes. I like the 23-inch-square size for banner making. They are available from many mail-order sources and local quilt shops. If you can't find one locally, recommend that your local quilt, fabric, or craft store carry them or see "Sources of Supplies" on page 91.

Pattern

Patterns are probably the most important notion of all. There are patterns designed specifically for banners, but don't let titles and descriptions on books and patterns mislead you. A pattern or design can be adapted to any area of creativity. An appliqué design can be used for making banners or doing cutwork. A quilting pattern can be scaled down and sewn to the front of a T-shirt or up to make a garden flag. You can also design your own patterns from ideas you may get from coloring books, calendars, greeting cards, and so forth. Be sure that any pattern you purchase has easy-to-follow instructions and is reusable. You'll find you can't make just one! As soon as friends and relatives see your new design, they will want one of their own. If your pattern is not reusable, you will need to purchase a new pattern for each banner that you make. This could get expensive.

When you choose a pattern, keep this in mind: Banner patterns should have simple, clean lines. A busy design is hard to understand from a distance. This is especially important with patterns for outdoor banners, which are usually viewed from a great distance, often from an automobile moving at 40 miles per hour. This does not allow the viewer much time to interpret your design. An indoor pattern can be more complex in nature, because viewers will have more time to look at and appreciate it.

Other Sewing Supplies and Helpful Notions

Sewing Machines

Of course, your sewing machine is your most important tool. I recommend one with a dependable tension system and an attractive zigzag satin stitch. You'll be most successful if you use a machine with which you are familiar. If your machine is not self-lubricating, keep it oiled. Be sure that it is tuned up and ready to go.

For successful machine appliqué, you'll need a presser foot for decorative stitching or appliqué. You'll find information on the special stitches and presser feet you'll need for the various techniques in Chapters 2 and 3.

If you have an older machine, do yourself a favor and visit your local sewing machine dealership. They can show you machines in any price range, and the new features and benefits offered on today's machines make sewing easy and more fun. If you are struggling with an old machine, you won't enjoy banner making or any other project. Having a good, reliable, trouble-free machine is a real plus.

Scissors

The most important notion in any sewing project is a good pair of sharp scissors. If you don't already own a quality pair of scissors, treat yourself to one. If you already have a good pair of sewing scissors, treat yourself to a pair of appliqué scissors. They are useful in banner making, cutwork, appliqué, quilting, and more. Appliqué scissors, shown in Figure 1.1, have a duck-billed blade that protects areas that you don't want to cut. They allow you to cut very close to the stitching line when trimming layers of fabric.

Figure 1.1

Needles

The thread and the fabric you are using will determine the type of needles you use. Appliqué on calico fabric using a standard cotton or polyester thread would require an 80/12 needle. Satin stitching on the 200 denier nylon with rayon thread requires a 90/14 stretch needle. You'll find any special recommendations for the needle style and size in the discussions of techniques used in each project.

Figure 1.2

Banner Tabs

Banner tabs, shown in Figure 1.2, are small pieces of leather that are sewn into the casing of outdoor banners to attach the banner to the pole it is displayed on. They keep the banner from sliding down the pole toward the bracket. These tabs are approximately 1 by 2 inches and have a buttonhole cut into one end, which you use to button your banner onto its pole. Some poles don't have a button or screw to button on a banner. In that case, simply tie your banner onto the pole by putting the tie through the buttonhole in the banner tab. Ty-Raps, used by electricians to hold bundles of wires, work great. They are relatively inexpensive and available at any hardware store. (See Fig. 1.3.)

Figure 1.3

Why not dress up a corner of your garden with a small garden flag? This sheep banner will add color and movement. Best of all, he won't eat any of your precious flowers. This banner was designed and sewn by Michele Shepler.

Mounting Hardware

As important as the banner itself is the manner in which it will be hung. After spending many long hours designing and sewing your banner, you will want to display it in the most attractive way possible.

Outdoor banners are displayed on wood, fiber glass or aluminum poles that either allow the banner to hang down vertically or tilt it at a slight angle. (See Fig. 1.4.) Banners are not mounted on a vertical pole like a flag. Some banner poles have a sleeve, called an unrapper tube, that fits over the pole, and the banner attaches to the sleeve. As the wind blows, the sleeve spins on the pole, but the banner always hangs free and never tangles. (See Fig. 1.5) You'll also need a bracket for your pole. I recommend an adjustable type that pivots 180 degrees. This allows you to mount your banner from either a horizontal or vertical surface. (See Fig. 1.6.) See "Sources of Supply" on page 91 for companies that sell poles for outdoor banners.

You can also display small decorative banners on garden flag poles, which are made from either wrought iron or wood. (See Fig. 1.7.) The banner is slipped onto a horizontal arm and the vertical post is then simply pushed into the ground anywhere in your lawn or garden. You can make your own wooden garden flag pole from dowel rods or purchase a wrought iron one.

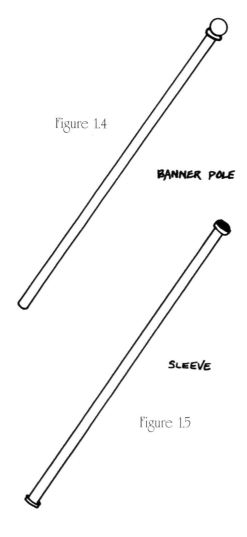

Figure 1.4

BANNER POLE

SLEEVE

Figure 1.5

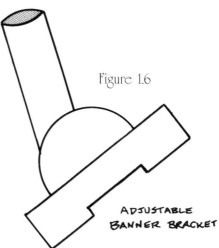

Figure 1.6

ADJUSTABLE BANNER BRACKET

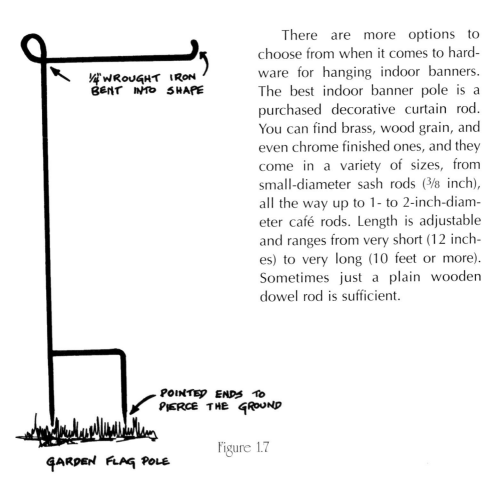

¼" WROUGHT IRON BENT INTO SHAPE

POINTED ENDS TO PIERCE THE GROUND

GARDEN FLAG POLE

Figure 1.7

There are more options to choose from when it comes to hardware for hanging indoor banners. The best indoor banner pole is a purchased decorative curtain rod. You can find brass, wood grain, and even chrome finished ones, and they come in a variety of sizes, from small-diameter sash rods (3/8 inch), all the way up to 1- to 2-inch-diameter café rods. Length is adjustable and ranges from very short (12 inches) to very long (10 feet or more). Sometimes just a plain wooden dowel rod is sufficient.

Chapter 2

Banner-Making Techniques

Celebrate your occupation or favorite hobby with a banner. This banner flies outside the sewing machine dealership that Elizabeth Carey manages. She asked artist Michele Shepler to design it for her. It's a great form of advertisement—sewers and non-sewers alike just love it.

There only are a few basic techniques you'll need to master to make any kind of banner. In this chapter, you'll find information on everything from enlarging your design to hemming and adding the casing to your banners. You'll also find directions for adding lettering. Appliqué is such an essential technique for banner making, it is covered in its own chapter, Chapter 3, beginning on page 25.

Enlarging and Reducing Designs

Full-size banner patterns are the easiest to work with, but you'll often have to enlarge or reduce pattern pieces for a banner before you start to make it. Since banners tend to be large, more often than not you'll need to enlarge a pattern rather than reduce it.

The fastest and easiest way to adjust the size of a design is on a copy machine. You can cut the original pattern up into smaller pieces and enlarge or reduce each one by the same percentage. Then tape the enlarged or reduced pieces together.

If you don't have access to a copy machine, you can use the grid enlargement method. To use a grid enlargement, lightly draw horizontal and vertical lines all over your pattern. Put them at 1/4-inch intervals on a small pattern and 1/2- to 3/4-inch intervals on a larger pattern. Then on a sheet of plain paper that is as large as you want your finished banner to be, draw a grid of horizontal and vertical lines at longer intervals. If you double the size of the grid on the paper (to 1/2-inch intervals for small patterns and 1- to 1 1/2-inch ones for larger patterns), you will double the size of the design for the finished banner.

Once you have drawn on your grid lines, use a pencil to copy the lines of the design from each square in the smaller grid into the corresponding squares in the larger grid. Work carefully, and make sure you transfer the design into the proper squares on the larger grid. You may find it helpful to number the grid sections horizontally and assign letters to the vertical sections, as shown in Figure 2.1. (This is the way grids on maps are labeled.)

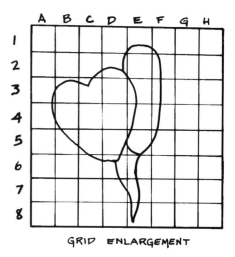

GRID ENLARGEMENT

Figure 2.1

The patterns in this book, which appear on page 93, already have a grid drawn over them. To enlarge them to the size called for in the

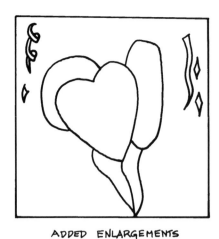

ADDED ENLARGEMENTS

Figure 2.2

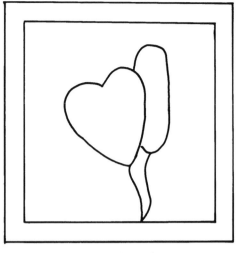

ADDED BORDER

Figure 2.3

directions, enlarge them on a copy machine until each grid square equals 1 inch, or draw then onto a 1-inch grid as explained above.

Another way to create a banner that's larger than your original pattern is to add pieces or accent features to the original design without enlarging the individual pieces in it. For example, you could trace an extra flower and add it to a floral design. Or, you could use a piece of background fabric that's larger than called for, and use decorative stitching to dress up the corners or fill in open space, as shown in Figure 2.2. You could also enlarge a banner by adding a border of contrasting fabric all around it, or just on three sides, as shown in Figure 2.3.

Hemming and Casing Construction

To finish the background fabric for your banner, you'll need to hem on three sides, and miter the corners when you turn them with your machine. You'll hem two long sides and one short side. The fourth short side is used to form a casing to hang your banner. Although the hemming and casing method described here was developed in our outdoor banner classes, it can be used for any type of banner with any type of fabric.

First, press in ½ to ⅝ inch on all four sides of the background piece. (See Fig. 2.4.) If you are using nylon fabric for an outdoor banner, use a medium heat silk/wool setting on your iron. Use steam and check the heat of your iron first on a scrap of the fabric. Nylon fabric will not form a sharp crease, but it will be visible

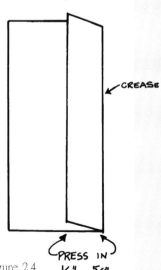

CREASE

Figure 2.4

PRESS IN
½" – ⅝"

No one could ever wonder who comes first in this household. This beautiful banner was sewn by Becky Beatty. She and husband, Bill, raise prize-winning collies. This exquisite banner is a real tribute to their beautiful dogs.

enough to work with. Do not try to turn your iron temperature up! That will only melt the nylon fabric.

Take your pressed fabric to your sewing machine, which should be threaded to match your background color. Finger press the raw edges in to meet the crease that you created with your iron, then fold in again on the pressed crease. (See Fig. 2.5.)

This will form approximately a 1/4-inch hem. Beginning at the top edge of the banner, hem down the right side first. Finger press as you go. Use a straight stitch with a standard stitch length, 2.5 to 3.0 mm or 10 to 12 stitches per inch. Stop sewing about 2 inches from the corner with the needle down in your fabric and follow the mitering instructions. (See Fig. 2.6.)

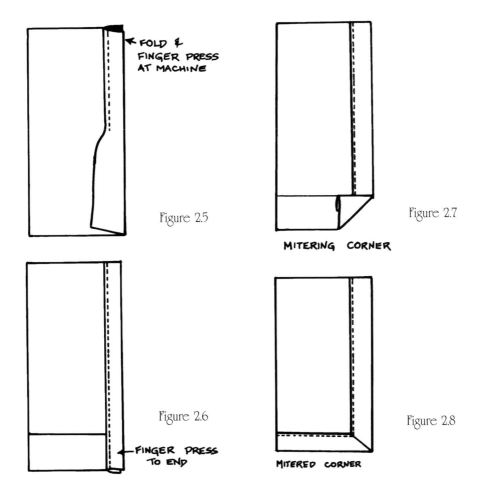

Figure 2.5

Figure 2.7

MITERING CORNER

Figure 2.6

Figure 2.8

MITERED CORNER

Mitering Corners

After stopping 2 inches from the corner, finish finger pressing the hem all the way to the edge. Fold the corner in to the left at a 45-degree angle so the folded edge of the long side lines up with the crease you pressed in on the short side. (See Fig. 2.7.) Then, as you did before, fold the raw edge of the short side in to meet the pressed crease, and fold in again on the pressed crease line.

Continue topstitching down to the miter until your needle drops into the fold of the miter. Now you can lift your presser foot and pivot your fabric so you can continue to hem across the short side of the background, as shown in Figure 2.8. When you drop your needle into the miter, it will hold the miter in place while you pivot your fabric—no need to use pins. Repeat the mitering procedure for the next corner and continue to topstitch the hem up the last long side, finger pressing as you go. Leave the top (the other short side) unhemmed. This is where you will create the casing for the banner pole.

Sewing the Casing

On the unhemmed short side, press in an additional 3 inches to form the casing for your pole. (See Fig. 2.9.) If you are making an outdoor banner, the next step is to sew in a banner tab to hold the banner on the pole. I like to use a 1 × 2-inch (approximately) leather banner tab to secure the banner to the pole. Place the tab with the edge of the slit end even with the hemmed side of the banner right at the 3-inch crease. (See Fig. 2.10.) On reversible banners it doesn't matter which side you sew it on; sew it on the back side if you are using these directions to case another type of banner. Use a leather needle in your sewing machine and sew it on with a rectangle and an "X." The slotted end of the tab should be free, not sewn down.

Once the tabs are in place, remove the leather needle and replace it with the needle you were using previously. (I use a 90/14 stretch needle on 200 denier nylon.) Using the thread that you hemmed with, sew the casing closed. Fold it down on the 3-inch crease line. Then tuck under the 1/2 to 5/8-inch strip you pressed on the raw edge, and topstitch it, just like the hem.

Strengthen the Hem and Casing

To strengthen the hem and casing, sew tiny bartacks over both miters and at the ends of the casing topstitching, as shown in Figure 2.11. These are the areas that are most likely to fray in the wind. To make a bartack, you will select a very narrow satin stitch, or select the automatic bartack stitch, if your machine has one.

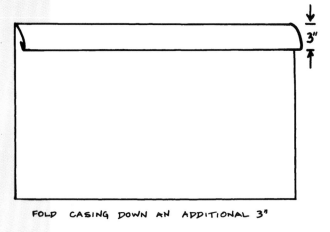

FOLD CASING DOWN AN ADDITIONAL 3"

Figure 2.9

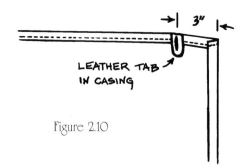

LEATHER TAB IN CASING

Figure 2.10

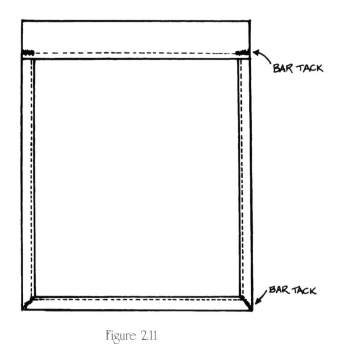

BAR TACK

BAR TACK

Figure 2.11

Free-Motion Quilting

Quilting can add depth and texture to a banner. To quilt a banner that you have finished appliquéing, you will need to line it and add some sort of batting or fleece. These layers need to be sandwiched together with the right sides of lining and the banner together and the batting on the lining side. Then sew around the edge and turn them to the right side. Before you start quilting, baste through all the layers to prevent shifting. The Angel Banner project on page 61 is machine quilted and contains more detailed instructions on preparing the banner for machine quilting.

The quickest way to quilt a design is to use free-motion quilting. You will need a machine that can lower the feed dogs or that comes equipped with a plate to cover the feed dogs. The next step is to loosen the pressure that is pressing down on the presser foot. Without feed dogs and pressure on the presser foot, the fabric is free to be moved anywhere you want to move it. If you have a darning foot or free-motion foot, use it. This is a foot that is spring-loaded in such a way that it only makes contact with the fabric when the needle is in the fabric. It lifts off the fabric when the needle rises up out of the fabric. This gives you the freedom to move the fabric anywhere you want to while maintaining good stitch quality. If you don't have access to a free-motion or darning foot, then use a standard straight stitching foot or a decorative stitching foot. Free-motion quilting work won't be as easy with these feet, but it can be done. Start by practicing on a scrap of fabric.

You will need to develop a rhythm for free-motion work. Because the machine is no longer feeding the fabric, you will have to decide how fast you need to run the machine and how fast you need to move the fabric to get the stitch length you want. Don't make the stitches too long. This comes from running the machine too slow and moving the fabric too fast. But on the other hand, if you run the machine too fast and the fabric too slow, the stitches will be too short. If you stitch too long in one spot, the thread could break. You will want to keep the machine and the movement of the fabric both at a steady even pace. If your machine has a speed control, turn it down to a slower speed. This way you can depress the foot pedal all the way down and only worry about varying the speed you're moving the fabric. When you are satisfied with the stitching sample you are working on, you can begin the banner.

Starting in an easy area, begin quilting. Remember to always put your presser foot down even though it really doesn't ride on the fabric. If your presser foot isn't down you won't have any tension on the upper thread and when you start to stitch your machine will jam, and threads will collect on the underside. Begin

Make a statement with a community service banner. This fused banner was designed and sewn by the author for her daughter Sally's Students Against Drunk Driving chapter. The banner was used to encourage students to sign an anti-drinking pledge during the Prom Promise campaign.

slowly, traveling along the edges of the areas that you want to accent with quilting. You may even quilt within a design piece to create texture. Try crisscross or swirling patterns with your quilting stitches. When you are satisfied with your quilting you can remove the basting stitches or pins.

Lettering

All banners have a message. Some messages are in the design only. A banner with a picture of Santa says Christmas, for example. But some messages need to be written. "Annual Strawberry Festival" or "Section Champions" are just two examples of lettering that might appear on a banner.

There are many ways to add lettering to a banner. It can be fused only, fused and appliquéd, satin stitched, and couched, to name a few techniques.

Lettering that will be fused or fused and appliquéd is prepared in the same manner. The only difference is the fusible product that is used. Trace letters to be fused only onto a heavy duty fusible that is intended for fusing only. It will bond strongly to the fabric, but cannot be sewn. Trace letters to be fused and then sewn onto a sewable, light-weight fusible. Always reverse letters when you trace them onto the fusible.

After tracing, iron the fusible to the wrong side of the lettering fabric, following the manufacturer's instructions. Then cut out the letters and peel away the paper backing. Place the cut-out letters in place on the banner and iron them on according to the manufacturer's instructions.

Some banners don't need words to communicate a message. This banner says Merry Christmas and Happy Holidays in any language. It beats a plastic light-up Santa any day. This banner was sewn by Sally Lowery.

If the letters are to be fused only, as they were on the Prom Promise Banner on page 22, they are finished. If they are to be appliquéd, sew around them using the techniques described in Chapter 3. See "Mastering Corners and Curves" on page 30.

Satin-stitched letters are just what the name implies—letters formed by satin stitching. Simply draw the letters on the banner using a removable marking pencil, and follow the lines with a satin stitch. Use the techniques I recommended for machine appliqué to stitch through outside corners, inside corners, and curves. See "Mastering Corners and Curves" on page 30.

Couched letters are formed by sewing over cords or braid following a lettering design that has been drawn with a removable marker. The lettering on the Strawberry Festival Banner project in Chapter 5 was created by sewing a three-step zigzag stitch over seven strands of pearl cotton with invisible thread. The seven strands of pearl cotton were threaded through the holes in a special foot. This seven hole cord foot lays the strands down perfectly while the machine stitches across them. Almost any stitch that is wide enough to cover the number of strands in your foot can be used. You may even choose to use a decorative or contrasting thread to couch over the strands in the foot.

Another type of couched lettering can be created with a braiding foot. This foot works in the same way as the seven hole foot. The difference is that the braiding foot has only one hole that can accommodate large braid or cording. Usually a zigzag with a width that just fits over the braid or cord is used to couch the lettering in place.

Chapter 3

Appliqué

Reversible appliqué banners like this stained-glass-window style rose design, are sewn with high-quality nylon fabric. The reversible appliqué technique makes it easy to sew a banner that's visible on both sides and only one fabric layer thick. This banner was designed and sewn by Michele Shepler.

Whether you are satin-stitching lettering, using your serger to outline a pattern piece, or sewing a reversible outdoor banner, you are using appliqué. In this chapter, you'll learn all about the machine appliqué techniques you need to become a master banner maker. The tech-niques described in the first part of the chapter, from page 27 to 33 apply to any type of machine appliqué. Following that, you'll find information on different types of appliqué, including complete instructions for making reversible outdoor banners.

Using Fusibles for Appliqué

In many cases, you'll want to fuse an entire appliqué design before you stitch to make sure the pattern pieces stay put. To fuse pattern pieces, you first need to trace the design pieces onto the fusing product. If it is important that your design faces the same direction as your pattern, you will need to use a tracing table or other tracing setup and turn your pattern face down while tracing onto the fusing product. If you don't, your design will be reversed when you are finished. This is especially important when you are working with lettering. Remember to use a fusing product that is intended for machine-sewn appliqué. The instructions that come with the product will show you how. See "Fusibles and Stabilizers for Fabric" on page 5 for more on types of fusibles.

When you have finished tracing the design pieces onto the paper backing of the fusing product fuse to the wrong side of the fabric you have chosen for each piece. Don't cut out the design you have traced onto the paper backing until it is fused to the fabric. Once it has been fused and has cooled, cut the paper backing and the fabric out at the same time. Then peel the paper from the back of the design pieces. Look closely and you will see the fusible web that has been transferred to the wrong side of your fabric.

Using your master pattern as a guide, pin the design pieces into place on the background fabric for your banner. When you are satisfied with the placement of your design, fuse the pieces into place with your iron, following the manufacturer's instructions.

Appliqué on Tricky Fabrics

Lightweight, silky, slippery, and loosely woven fabrics are sometimes difficult to appliqué. They can bunch, slide, pucker, and ravel. The secret to success with these fabrics is to prepare them properly.

Paper-backed fusible web and proper stabilization will solve all the problems of working with these fabrics. The fusible will hold the design piece securely to the background and prevent bunching, sliding, and raveling. The stabilizer will prevent puckering and tunneling. Some fabrics, like tissue lamé are so fine they can't support an appliqué stitch on their own. For fabrics like these, fuse muslin to the wrong side with a paper-backed fusible to provide extra support. Then use paper backed fusible again to fuse the muslin backing to the background. The fine, tight weave of the muslin will prevent the edge of the lamé from slipping off.

What if you don't want the entire design piece to be fused down? You can fuse only the edges of the design piece by stitching around it with fusible thread in the bobbin. This will place just one stitching line of fusing area on the wrong side of the design piece. Then you can fuse only the edges of the design to the background fabric. (Be sure to follow manufacturer's instructions when using these products.) Stabilize the area and appliqué with a stitch that is wide enough to cover the edge of the design piece as well as the line of fusible thread stitching.

Machine Appliqué Techniques

For successful appliqué, you need a decorative stitching or appliqué foot. This is a presser foot that has a channel underneath that allows the foot to glide over the raised satin stitching. A standard straight-stitch foot is perfectly flat on the bottom and will not move over satin stitching easily. Some sewing machines have an open-toe appliqué foot. This foot has no bar across the sewing area. Therefore, it does not obstruct your view in any way. For illustrations of these presser feet, see Figures 3.1, 3.2, and 3.3.

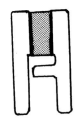

BOTTOM - DECORATIVE FOOT

Figure 3.2

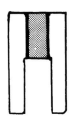

BOTTOM - OPEN TOE FOOT

Figure 3.3

The stitch you select will depend on the type of appliqué you have chosen. Depending on the project and the machine you have, you may select a zigzag stitch, an heirloom

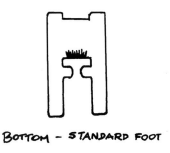

BOTTOM - STANDARD FOOT

Figure 3.1

Whether you love bowling, croquet, or golf, you can commemorate your sport with a banner. This banner announces the author's father and stepmother's favorite hobby. It's extra-special because an 8-year-old friend named Cori Shepler made it. She has made quite a few other banners already as well.

appliqué stitch (also called a blanket stitch or a buttonhole stitch, depending on your machine), or a seam-and-overcast stitch. You'll find recommendations for specific stitches below and in the project chapters later in the book. Use a width that is suitable for your design. If the design is small and intricate, you wouldn't want a stitch that is ³/₈- to ¼-inch

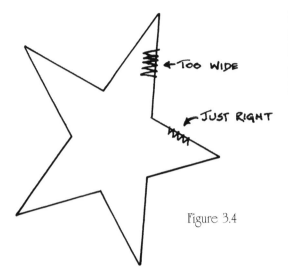

Figure 3.4

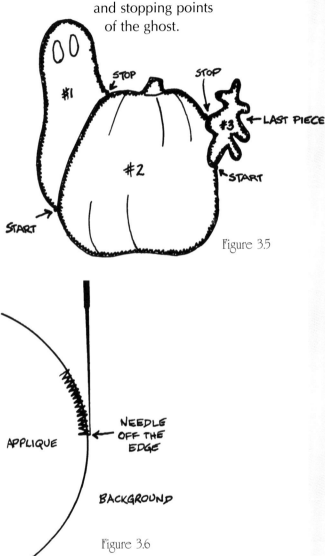

piece to appliqué first. Start with the ghost, beginning and ending where he touches the pumpkin. Then stitch all around the pumpkins. The pumpkin stitching will seal off the starting and stopping points of the ghost.

Figure 3.5

wide (4.5 to 6 mm). (See Fig. 3.4.) Then adjust the stitch length so the stitches are as close together as you want them to be. The length could be longer on fabrics that don't ravel and shorter on fabrics that do. Always test your stitch on a scrap piece first.

Now you are ready to decide which piece to sew on first. I always begin with the part of the design that seems to be farthest away. After appliquéing that piece, I keep working forward in my design until I reach the foreground, or the piece that seems closest. This not only lets you avoid redundant stitching, it also allows you to cross the beginning and the end of stitching lines of earlier pieces as you add on new ones. As new stitching lines cross the ones that are already there, they lock in the loose ends you get at starting and stopping points. See Figure 3.5, which shows part of the Halloween banner project from Chapter 7, for an example of this process. You can see clearly which

Figure 3.6

When you appliqué, the stitching should be almost entirely on the appliqué design piece, with the needle going just barely off the edge into the background fabric. (See Fig. 3.6.) Stitching along a straight line or a long smooth curve is not a problem. You will be able to guide your fabric by lining it up with a spot on your presser foot. To start sewing, select a straight section of your design and put your needle into the background fabric at the edge of the design piece. Then put your presser foot down and select a spot on it that you can use as a visual guide while you sew. This is the spot I watch while I sew, not the needle. (See Fig. 3-7.) You can mark the spot on the presser foot with a Sharpie marker. Start out slowly, until you are comfortable with what you are doing. Speed will come with practice.

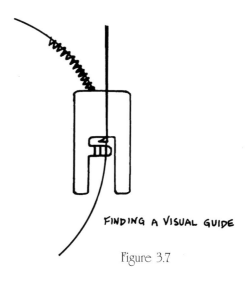

FINDING A VISUAL GUIDE

Figure 3.7

Mastering Corners and Curves

Appliqué is easy once you have mastered sewing along three types of edges: Outside corners, inside corners, and curves. Mastering them is the key to professional-looking results. A neatly turned corner and a smooth, even curve is what you are striving for. Follow these simple instructions to achieve professional results.

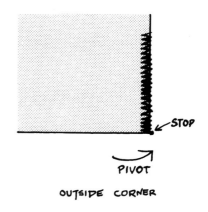

STOP

PIVOT

OUTSIDE CORNER

Figure 3.8

Outside Corners

When you sew up to an outside corner, the technique for turning it becomes obvious. Because you are stitching with the needle falling just off the edge of the fabric, you will stop with the needle exactly at the point of the outside corner, as shown in Figure 3.8. If you continue stitching any further, you will leave the design piece and enter the background fabric only. If your sewing machine has a needle-down feature, use it. It's a great time-saver when appliquéing. When the needle stops down in the fabric, just lift the presser foot and pivot. If you don't have a needle-down feature, you'll need to turn the hand wheel to put the needle in the fabric at the point of the outside corner, then lift the presser foot and turn the fabric before you can stitch down the adjoining side.

Show how proud you are of your heritage with an outdoor banner featuring your family crest or the flag of your ancestors' homeland. This banner of the flag of Wales was sewn by Marty Worthington for her husband Eric.

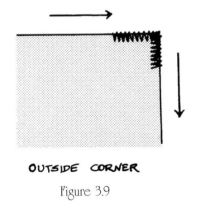

OUTSIDE CORNER

Figure 3.9

(See Fig. 3.9) As you continue sewing, make sure the needle drops barely off the edge of the design piece into the background fabric, as it did before.

The technique described above works well on corners of 90 degrees or more. For corners of less than 90 degrees, you'll need to use a different technique. There are two ways you can turn these narrow corners. For the first method, narrow your zigzag or satin stitch as you approach the corner, as shown in Figure 3.10. Then pivot at the corner

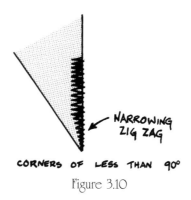

NARROWING ZIG ZAG

CORNERS OF LESS THAN 90°

Figure 3.10

as you would normally, and as you start sewing along the next edge, gradually widen the stitch as you go away from the corner. The second method is probably easier: Stop stitching when you are as far away from the corner as the width of your stitch. Turn your fabric so that you will stitch across the point at a right angle for only a few stitches. When the point is covered, pivot again, and stitch down the other side, as shown in Figure 3.11.

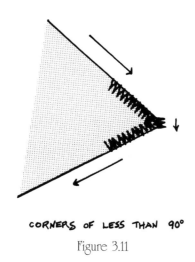

CORNERS OF LESS THAN 90°

Figure 3.11

Inside Corners

Inside corners are appliquéd in much the same way as outside cor-

ners. The pivot point is at the corner, but you pivot when the needle is down in the appliqué piece, not in the background fabric. As you reach the inside corner, continue to stitch past the corner into the design piece a distance that is equal to the width of your stitch. Stop with the needle down in the appliqué piece, and then lift the presser foot and pivot your fabric, as shown in Figure 3.12. Continue sewing down the adjoining side with the needle dropping into the background at the edge of the design piece. Sew inside corners that are less than 90 degrees the same way you would sew outside corners of less than 90 degrees.

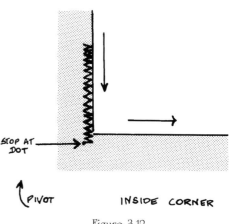

STOP AT DOT

PIVOT

INSIDE CORNER

Figure 3.12

Curves

Poorly turned curves are a dead giveaway to amateur appliqué. A common mistake is trying to steer around a sharp curve without stopping to pivot the fabric. This results in slanted stitches. (See Fig. 3.13.) The solution to this problem is to stop and pivot every few stitches around the curve. This may seem

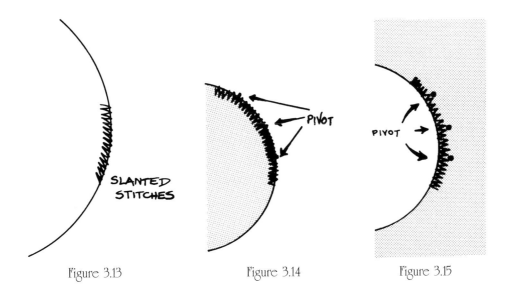

Figure 3.13   Figure 3.14   Figure 3.15

tedious, but is certainly worth it. Whether you are sewing an inside curve or an outside curve, as you approach it, begin turning the fabric gradually so that your needle continues to drop off the edge of the design piece into the background fabric. As the curve increases, you will need to stop with the needle down in the fabric on the outside of the curve, lift your presser foot, pivot the fabric slightly, lower presser foot, and begin stitching again. Repeat this process until you have completed the curve. Figures 3.14 and 3.15 show examples of both inside and outside curves sewn with this technique. Remember, practice makes perfect, so don't get discouraged on your first project.

Types of Appliqué

There are several different appliqué techniques you can use to create banners, including everything from satin stitch to no-sew appliqué. I use reversible appliqué to make outdoor banners because the technique makes it possible to create a lightweight banner that is only one layer of fabric thick. Sunlight shines through these banners, which I make from nylon fabric, and makes the colors in them literally glow. For directions on reversible appliqué banners, see "Reversible Appliqué" on page 39.

Satin Stitch Appliqué

Satin stitch appliqué is the type used most frequently. It is a zigzag with a very short stitch length. Some of the computerized machines have a built in satin stitch appliqué. This stitch is formed so that the stitch remains smooth, even when going around curves. It reduces the amount of pivoting needed.

What can be more cause for celebration than a graduation? This banner says "hats off" to a job well done. You can even add extra accents that are symbolic of activities or achievements your special graduate accomplished. This banner was sewn by the author for her daughter's high school graduation. The music notes recognize her achievements with the marching band.

To set your machine for satin stitch appliqué, select a zigzag with a very short stitch length. The width of the zigzag will be determined by the size of the appliqué design. Follow the directions given above sewing inside and outside corners as well as curves.

Shaded Stitch Appliqué

You may want to use shaded stitch appliqué to avoid the sharp lines of normal satin stitched appliqué. (I used this stitch on the face and hands of the Angel Banner in Chapter 6.) Some computerized sewing machines have this stitch built in, but it can be programmed into a computerized machine that doesn't have it, if the machine has a left or right needle zigzag. (If you don't have a computerized sewing machine you'll need to just use a regular satin stitch.)

Put your machine into program. Select either the left or right needle position zigzag stitch. Select the stitch width that you want for the first stitch, and set the stitch length to satin stitch. Now enter the stitch. Select the same left or right needle zigzag and select a new width for the second stitch. Set the length for satin stitch and enter the stitch. Continue the process changing the stitch width for each stitch, but leaving the length on satin stitch. After you have programmed about 15 to 20 stitches, you can put your design into repeat. Then this series of stitch-

SHADED APPLIQUE STITCH

Figure 3.16

es will repeat over and over. You will get a satin stitch with one side even and the other side with varying widths while the stitch length will remain the same. (See Fig. 3.16.)

Serger Appliqué

Serger appliqué is a quick and easy way to make indoor banners— I used it on the Strawberry Festival Banner in Chapter 5. To use your serger for banner making, set it up for a rolled hem. You will be using only one needle, probably a rolled hem foot, and possibly a rolled hem throat plate. Refer to your owner's manual for complete instructions. Usually you will need to adjust your tensions for a rolled hem. The lower or under looper tension will be turned to a higher number, or tightened considerably. The upper or over looper sometimes needs to be tightened slightly. The needle tension usually remains at the normal setting. If you have any questions the owner's manual should answer them.

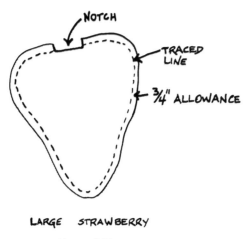

LARGE STRAWBERRY

Figure 3.17

Begin by cutting the traced design from the main fabric piece, leaving approximately ¾ inch all around the traced line. Then cut a piece out along the top edge to create a starting and stopping point, as shown in Figure 3.17. Choose a point that would be covered by the other design pieces later, if possible. The piece should be about 1½ to 2 inches long. Precutting this "notch" allows you to start and stop with your blade even with the traced line. You also won't have to run on and run off at an angle when starting and stopping your rolled hem. After testing the rolled hem on a scrap of your design fabric, begin serging at the notch you just cut. Serge a rolled hem all around the outside with the blade cutting just outside of the

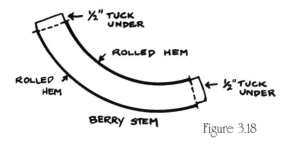

BERRY STEM

Figure 3.18

traced chalk line. Allow a little extra room, approximately ½ inch, on design pieces that will be tucked under other design pieces, such as the berry stems on the Strawberry Festival Banner, as shown in Figure 3.18. Remember to run the cutting blade just outside of the traced chalk lines.

Stitch design pieces that have been finished with a rolled hem into place using a piping foot or a zipper foot. The groove under the piping foot will ride along the rolled hem edge allowing you to stitch up close to the rolled hem stitching. If you don't have a piping foot, your zipper foot will allow you to stitch up close to the rolled hem stitching. This is sometimes referred to as stitching in the ditch.

Invisible Appliqué

For creating a hand sewn look or making a banner when you want the design to stand out, not the appliqué stitching, invisible or hidden appliqué is a good choice. The first step in this technique is to trace the design pieces onto the wrong side of the design fabric. Use a tracing table for this if you have one. There are two ways to finish invisible appliqué. The first is to cut the pieces out ¼ inch outside the traced lines, and press the extra ¼ inch to the wrong side. Or you may choose to place another piece of the design fabric under the traced piece, right sides together, then stitch and turn them as follows. You can also add a layer of batting or fleece on the bot-

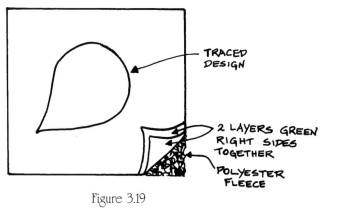

Figure 3.19

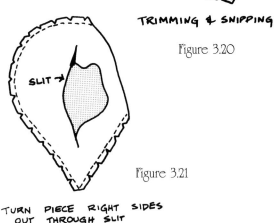

TRIMMING & SNIPPING

Figure 3.20

SLIT →

Figure 3.21

TURN PIECE RIGHT SIDES
OUT THROUGH SLIT

tom, under the fabric you added, and sew it in for a quilted look, as shown in Figure 3.19.

Once you've sandwiched your layers, stitch all the way around the design with a short, straight stitch. Then trim the seams: You may need to snip in close to the seam on curves and trim corners to make turning easier. (See Fig. 3.20.) Next, cut a slit in the top layer of fabric big enough to turn the design to the right side of the fabric. (See Fig 3.21.) Use a long, thin object through the hole that you cut to gently push any points into place. Make sure that the object you are using is thin but blunt. A sharp tool will poke a hole in your fabric. There are various point-turning tools on the market, including the Stuff-It tool, the Collar and Point Turner (it resembles a pair of scissors), or the Bamboo Point Turner. Check at your local sewing supply store or see "Sources of Supplies" on page 91.

Now you have a design piece that is finished all the way around. Stitch the slit that was cut closed by hand. You may appliqué all the way around the design piece, or leave part of the piece free for a three dimensional design. The leaves and blossom on the Strawberry Festival Banner project in Chapter 5 were sewn in this manner.

A fine monofilament nylon thread is ideal for hidden appliqué. The .004 mm size is the easiest to work with. It is as fine as a hair on your head and very easy to work with. There are some invisible threads on the market that are as coarse as fishing line: Don't buy this type. Fellow sewers who say they never work with invisible thread because it is stiff, coarse, and cranky, are talking about this coarser thread. I have introduced dozens of people to the fine invisible thread, and when they try it, they can't believe it. It is usually available from mail order sources or specialty sewing shops. You will recognize it because it comes on a small cone, not a spool like the coarser ones. The only thing you need to be aware of is that if you overfill a plastic bobbin with monofilament nylon thread, it could break. Because this thread is so fine, even a half-filled bobbin lasts a very long time. So I only fill my plastic bobbins about half full to be safe.

The .004 size comes in two colors: clear for light fabrics and smoke for dark fabrics. You can find it at your local specialty sewing shop or see "Sources of Supply" on page 91. Brands to ask for are Wonder Thread or YLI .004 monofilament nylon.

Set your sewing machine for a narrow zigzag, a seam-and-overcast stitch, or heirloom appliqué stitch, also called a blanket or buttonhole stitch. (See Fig. 3.22.) You will want the stitch to be narrow enough to just barely catch the edge of the appliqué design while stitching into the background fabric, just at the design's edge. Usually the width will be set for 1 to 1.5 mm.

You may want to begin stitching with the needle just catching the edge of the design piece. Using the

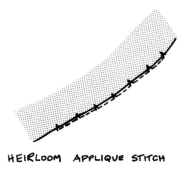

HEIRLOOM APPLIQUE STITCH

Figure 3.22

hand wheel, move the needle to the opposite side of its swing. Adjust the width until it goes into the background fabric at the edge of the design piece. The .004 mm monofilament is so fine that you may have trouble seeing the stitches. Now you know why it is called hidden or invisible appliqué.

No-Sew Appliqué

Not all banner designs have to be appliquéd. Fabrics that resist raveling like felt, Ultrasuede, and tightly woven cottons can be used very effectively for no-sew appliqué. Some fusing products are intended to be fused only. The fusing agent is strong and cannot be sewn. Simply trace the design pieces onto the paper backing of the fusing product, iron the product onto the back of the design fabrics, cut out the design, remove the paper backing, and fuse into place on the background fabric. As always, follow manufacturer's instructions.

Garden flags are merely banners on a smaller scale. They are quick to make and add a little sparkle to any garden. Use them to decorate for holidays or just as nice accents for a summer lawn. This garden flag was designed and sewn by Michele Shepler.

Reversible Appliqué

Banners that will be viewed from both sides need to be reversible. This appliqué technique allows you to create a banner that is only one layer of fabric thick. Unlike banners with multiple layers of fabric, which are dark and heavy, reversible appliqué banners are light and airy. They are especially attractive when the sun shines through them.

All three of the outdoor banner projects in this book are constructed with reversible appliqué (Chapter 7, Halloween Banner; Chapter 8, Sunflower Banner; and Chapter 9, Baby Carriage Banner). Follow the steps below to make a professional looking banner that is fully reversible.

Selecting the Size of the Banner

The outdoor banners made with reversible appliqué in this book are 30 by 45 inches in size. I chose that size because the 200 denier nylon fabric from which they are constructed is 60 inches wide. That means when you purchase 1¼ yards (45 inches) of it, you can split the fabric down the middle and create two backgrounds. (See Fig. 3.23.) If you want to make a banner

that is 36 by 60 inches, then you would have to purchase exactly 1 yard.

On thing to look for before you proceed with your banner is whether or not your design pieces extend into the hemmed edge of your banner. When designs extend over the hem, the banner is appliquéd first and hemmed last. If the design pieces either stay inside the hem, as they do on the Halloween Banner, or fall off the edge of the banner, as they do on the Baby Carriage Banner, you will need to hem your background before you appliqué.

Trace the Design

If you are using the patterns in this book, you will need to enlarge them to the finished size that you want. See "Enlarging and Reducing Designs" on page 16 for directions. When you are satisfied with the size you have, begin tracing. To trace, simply place each color of nylon over the pattern, one color at a time. Using a chalk marker, trace each area of the design onto the color for that area. Make sure you trace every detail and feature. When tracing more than one part of the design onto the same color of fabric, be sure to leave at least ½ inch between the pieces so you will be able to cut

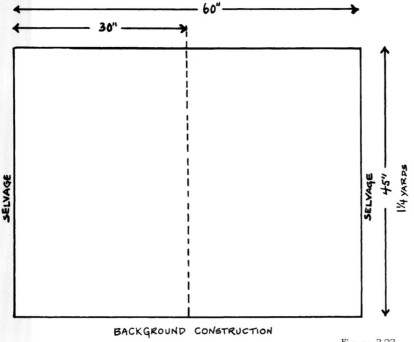

BACKGROUND CONSTRUCTION

Figure 3.23

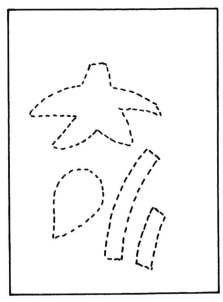

TRACING WITH DOTTED LINES

Figure 3.24

them out later. (See Fig 3.24.) If the nylon fabric is a color that is too dark to see through, you will need to use a tracing table or other light source.

Do not cut these pieces out yet!

Outline Stitch the Pieces

Fusible thread is the secret to making a fully reversible banner that is only one layer thick. The pieces of your design are stitched with fusible thread, then fused together like a puzzle. Here's how it works:

Fill a bobbin with fusible thread. Because this thread is so thick (it looks like dental floss) your bobbin will fill very quickly. If your sewing machine does not have an automatic shut off, be sure not to overfill the bobbin. Thread the top of your machine with the color of rayon

thread you will be appliquéing with later. I prefer rayon thread to any other type of thread for this purpose. The colors of rayon are the most brilliant, and it has a beautiful sheen. If you don't want to use rayon thread, you don't have to, though.

Set your sewing machine for a straight stitch, basting stitch length. Now tighten your upper tension just slightly, usually 1 to 2 numbers higher than the standard setting you use for a good balanced stitch. If you don't tighten the upper tension when you use fusible thread, it will pull the top thread to the bottom of the fabric. As a result, the fusible thread will run nearly straight along the bottom. (See Fig 3.25.) The fusible thread won't fuse properly unless you tighten the tension so the upper thread pulls it into a more balanced stitch. Start stitching on the exterior lines of your design pieces. Stitch right on top of the traced chalk lines. Remember: exterior lines only. Do not stitch with fusible thread on any of the accent or feature lines. (See Fig 3.26.)

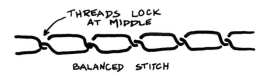

THREADS LOCK AT MIDDLE

BALANCED STITCH

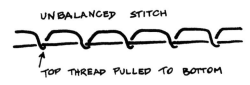

UNBALANCED STITCH

TOP THREAD PULLED TO BOTTOM

Figure 3.25

DON'T STITCH ON
FEATURE LINES

STITCH ON
TRACED LINES

Figure 3.26

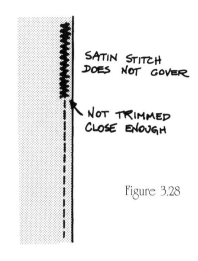

SATIN STITCH
DOES NOT COVER

NOT TRIMMED
CLOSE ENOUGH

Figure 3.28

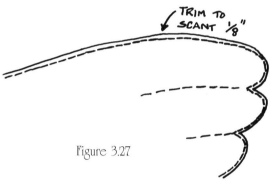

TRIM TO
SCANT ⅛"

Figure 3.27

Trim the Pieces

When all design pieces are traced and stitched with the fusible thread, cut them out using a good sharp pair of scissors. Appliqué scissors work great. When you cut, stay a scant ⅛ inch outside of the stitching line. (See Fig. 3.27.) Be careful: If you cut more than ⅛ inch, the appliqué satin stitching will not cover the fusible thread stitching line and the raw edge of the design piece. (See Fig. 3.28.) If you cut less than ⅛ inch, you run the risk of either cutting the stitching line or having the stitches slip off the edge.

This is a step in the process of banner making that takes patience.

If you are nervous about cutting all of your pieces out and fusing them together at one time, you can fuse some of the smaller pieces together before you assemble the entire banner. The brown centers can be sewn inside the yellow petals of the sunflowers in the Sunflower Banner this way: See "Piecing Your Sunflower" on page 82 for more on this technique.

Position and Fuse the Design

You'll need to have a hemmed and cased piece of background fabric for this next step. If you don't already have one, turn to "Hemming and Casing Construction" on page 17.

Lay the paper pattern down with the right side up. Place your hemmed-and-cased background over the pattern so that the design is where you want it to be. Begin pinning the stitched-and-trimmed design pieces into place on the background, using the paper pattern as the guide. Dark color backgrounds are hard to see through. You may want to take this into consideration when selecting your background color. If your design pieces have been traced, stitched, and cut accurately, they should fit together like a puzzle. The 1/8-inch margin left on the outside of each traced and stitched line allows you approximately 1/4-inch overlap on all pieces. The lines of fusible thread stitching on adjoining pieces should lay right on top of each other. (See Fig. 3.29.) When all the pieces are in place, you are ready to fuse them to the background.

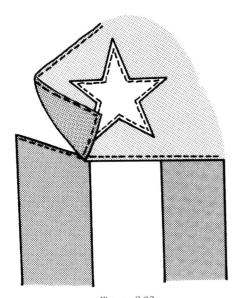

Figure 3.29

When fusing, use as much heat and steam as your fabric will allow. I like to use the maximum (cotton) setting on my iron, while protecting the nylon fabric with a muslin press cloth. Always test your iron temper-

ature on a scrap of nylon with a pressing cloth. This is the only way you can be sure that you are safe. Remember: nylon fabric melts!

Press each section by placing the iron down in one spot, using the pressing cloth. Do not slide the iron around. This could cause the appliqué design pieces to shift. Hold the iron in one spot for a few seconds, then move to a new area and repeat the pressing process. After the entire design has been warmed and the fusible thread seems to be adhering, you will need to repeat the same process using the steam burst feature of your iron, if you have one. If you don't have a steam burst, simply let your iron rest for a few seconds in each area with a maximum steam setting. Let the banner cool completely before continuing on. When the fusible thread is warm, it tends to be gummy and can pull away.

Stabilize the Banner

Decide which type of stabilizer you want to use and follow the manufacturer's instructions. See "Stabilizers" on page 6 for more on these products. In addition to your banner, also stabilize a couple of scrap pieces of fabric for practicing. For nylon fabric I would recommend either a fusible tearaway stabilizer or a spray-on stabilizer. Because the nylon fabric is slippery, you need a stabilizer that stays with the banner in the sewing machine. A regular tearaway or heat-away stabilizer would shift and bunch when you try to appliqué it. If you decide to use the iron-on tear away, set your iron to a silk/wool setting or less. Do not overheat the stabilizer. The nylon could melt and cause the stabilizer to fuse permanently. You can always warm it again. Don't overdo it the first time. Once your banner is stabilized you are ready to appliqué your design.

Set Your Machine

Remove the fusible thread from the bobbin of your machine and replace it with a bobbin filled with the rayon thread with which you are going to appliqué. Put an open-toe appliqué or decorative stitching foot on your machine if you have one. Set your machine for a medium zigzag width. I also recommend using a 90/14 stretch needle for satin stitching on the 200 denier nylon. Since you will be appliquéing again from the other side with a wider stitch, you can't use the widest setting now. Set the stitch length so that the stitches are close together but not satiny. (See Fig. 3.30.) Stitches that are too dense here make it difficult to stitch on the other side. You will hang up on curves and corners. Be sure to lower your upper tension

CLOSE BUT
NOT SATIN

STITCHES
TOO DENSE

Figure 3.30

so that you get a smooth stitch. The bobbin threads should always pull slightly to the back and should not show on top.

Before you start sewing on your banner, practice on one of your stabilized scraps. When you begin to appliqué your banner, be sure to sew around only the exterior lines of each design piece. As you sew, use the techniques I recommended in "Mastering Corners and Curves" on page 30. Do not sew any detail or feature lines yet. If you used the iron-on tearaway stabilizer, tear it away after you've finished appliquéing. Pull it toward the stitching while tearing it off. This leaves as little of the product behind as possible. (See Fig. 3.31.)

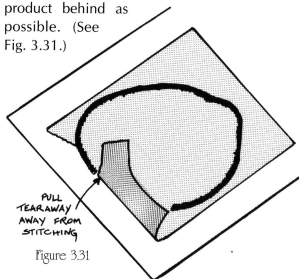

PULL
TEARAWAY
AWAY FROM
STITCHING

Figure 3.31

Trim the Background

To make your banner design visible from both sides, you must trim the background fabric away from the back of the appliqué. This can be a little tricky, so take your time. If you don't already own appliqué scissors, now would be a good time

Banners make beautiful indoor accents, too. Reversible appliqué banners like this stained-glass-window style one will add color to any room during the daylight hours. At night, it adds extra privacy and shines through for passers-by to enjoy. This banner was designed and sewn by Michele Shepler.

to purchase them. The duck billed blade of the appliqué scissors protects the stitching line and the appliqué piece while you trim. You can use them with the duck bill on top to protect the stitching line, or underneath, to protect the appliqué piece.

To trim, lay the banner flat and slip the scissors in between the layers. (See Fig 3.32.) Be careful to cut only the background layer. Hold the scissors with the blades flat on the banner, not perpendicular like normal scissors. The handles are bent to raise your hand up away from the

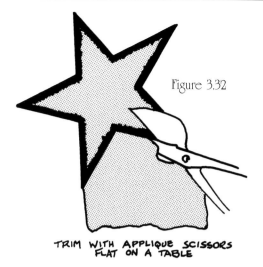

Figure 3.32

TRIM WITH APPLIQUE SCISSORS
FLAT ON A TABLE

stitch because the stitches on the back will fill in the spaces left by the stitches on the front. The finished result looks

STITCHING SLIGHTLY WIDER ON BACK

Figure 3.33

cutting surface. You can hold the scissors with your palm up or palm down. When trimming a large or intricate design, I keep changing my hand position from palm up to palm down. If you accidentally slip and cut your stitching or appliqué piece, you will probably be able to repair it when you stitch on the other side.

Reverse the Appliqué

Now, using the same colors of thread that you used to appliqué on the front of the banner, satin stitch again on the back. You will not need to add more stabilizer this time. The lines of satin stitching from the front will provide enough support as you stitch from the back. You will need to set your sewing machine for a zigzag stitch that is slightly wider than the one you used on the front. (See Fig 3.33.) Don't make the difference in width too great. A stitch that is too wide will cause the fabric to pinch in. Keep the stitch length the same as before or just slightly longer. You don't need a very satiny

like a smooth satin stitch. Use the same techniques for outside corners, inside corners, and curves that were discussed earlier.

Stitch Accent Lines and Features

Working from the front side again, where your chalk markings are, satin stitch any accent or feature lines, using rayon thread in both the top and bobbin of your machine. You will be stitching on only one layer of fabric, so be sure it is properly stabilized. Add another piece of iron-on tear away to the back of the accent stitching area, if that is the type of stabilizer that you are using. If you are using spray-on stabilizer, you may need to add a little more. Do whatever you need to keep the fabric from pinching or tunneling as you stitch. If you set your machine for a more satiny stitch, with a shorter stitch length, you won't have to stitch the accent lines again from the back. Of course you may restitch them, if you wish. If you do stitch them again from the back, you won't need to use stabilizer.

Chapter 4

Felt Sports Championship Banner

Whether you need a banner to carry in front of a marching band or hang in a gymnasium, no-sew appliqué is a good choice for constructing it. This banner was designed and made by author Ruth Ann Lowery.

Indoor Banner

Technique:

No-Sew Appliqué

Finished Size:

24 by 48 inches (2 × 4 feet)

Fabric and Supplies:

27 by 48-inch piece of felt for background

3/8 yard felt for letters and mascot

3/4 yard no-sew fusible web

High school gymnasiums, pools, and stadiums sport banners like this one celebrating the home team. This design is quite simple—it just proclaims the home team is the section champion. Those two words and your school mascot say it all. Your team is the best, and you are proud of them.

I made this banner from a good-quality felt. Because felt does not ravel, and the banner will be hung indoors, I decided fusing the design was a good choice. The no-sew fusibles available are very strong and reliable.

Constructing the Banner

To make your own sports banner, follow the step by step instructions below. You'll find the pattern for the mascot on this banner in "Patterns" on page 92, along with directions for enlarging it to the size you need to follow the directions given here.

1. Decide how large you want your finished banner to be. For this banner, I selected a finished size of 2 by 4 feet, with 3-inch lettering, and allowed approximately 12 inches for the mascot. I added 3 inches to the height of the finished size for the casing before cutting the background. (My background fabric was originally 27 by 48 inches. After I turned down my 3-inch casing, the finished size was 24 by 48 inches.) Usually a 3-inch casing is sufficient to fit over any pole you may use.

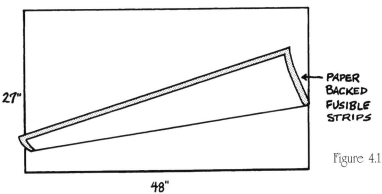

PAPER BACKED FUSIBLE STRIPS

Figure 4.1

27"

48"

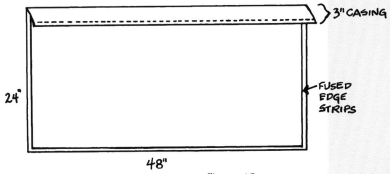

3" CASING

24"

FUSED EDGE STRIPS

48"

Figure 4.2

2. Finish the bottom and side edges of the banner background. You can fuse strips of matching background fabric on the underside to stabilize the edges, using a no-sew fusible. If you have a serger you can finish all the edges with a 3- or 4-thread overlock stitch using matching or contrasting thread. The last option would be to use your sewing machine to turn under and topstitch the edge. I chose to fuse my edges, because it is quick, easy, and neat. (See Fig. 4.1.)

3. Make the casing along the top edge of the background. (Remember to be sure that the casing is going to fit over the banner pole.) To create the casing I ironed a narrow strip of the fusible product to the back edge of the top of the banner. After removing the paper backing from the fusible product. I turned the top edge down 3 inches and pressed it to the back of the banner. (See Fig. 4.2.)

4. Now you are ready to create your design. If you choose, as I did, to only fuse your design, purchase a no-sew fusible that will

bond well. (Remember you cannot stitch through these products.) Trace or draw your letters and mascot onto the paper backing on the fusible. When working with a fusible, remember that everything must be reversed. If you are using a purchased tagboard stencil for your lettering, remember to turn it over and trace your letters backwards. (Some letters, of course, are the same when reversed.) The mascot needs to be drawn or traced facing the opposite direction that it will face on the finished banner. The fusibles are very transparent. If you have access to a light table, you can place your original artwork face down on the light table. Then lay the fusible over it with the paper side up. You should still be able to see the design enough to trace it. This method will reverse the letters and designs for you.

5. Press the fusible to the back of the fabric you have chosen for the letters and design. Don't cut the traced pieces out until they have been fused. To fuse, place the fusible product—paper side up—onto the wrong side of your design fabric. Press the fusible into place, according to manufacturer's instructions.

6. After the fusible cools, cut the letters and design pieces out. Remove the paper backing from the pieces you have cut out and begin placing them onto the background. When you are satisfied that all of your pieces are where you want them to be, fuse them to the background according to the manufacturer's instructions.

Chapter 5

Annual Strawberry Festival Banner

Don't let anyone forget that festival you've worked so hard on—remind them it's just around the corner with a banner like this one. This banner was designed by Michele Shepler and sewn by author Ruth Ann Lowery.

Indoor Banner

Technique:

Serger and Invisible Appliqué

Finished size:

30 by 72 inches (approximately)

Fabrics and Supplies:

Fabric requirements are given in yardage first. The measurements in parentheses are the actual dimensions needed. This will make it easy to use scraps of fabric you have at home.

2 yards for background

2 yards for lining

2 yards polyester fleece

½ yard red print for strawberries (18 × 30 inches)

½ yard green print for vines and leaves (18 × 30 inches)

¼ yard white for blossom (9 × 9 inches)

A scrap of yellow for blossom center

Threads of your choice for appliqué. I choose black rayon thread for serger appliqué and monofilament nylon .004 mm for the invisible appliqué. The lettering was done with strands of dark green pearl cotton.

Piping or zipper foot

7-hole cord foot (optional)

Annual strawberry festivals are popular community events from coast to coast. Whether hosted by a church, ladies auxiliary, or local garden club, they are a reminder of childhood days back home. Since community celebrations and quilts are both symbols of hearth and home, I chose a quilt-like design for my Strawberry Festival Banner.

On my banner, the strawberries and stems are sewn on using serger appliqué. If you don't have a serger, you can use one of the appliqué techniques described in Chapter 3: Satin stitch is a good choice for both. (See page 33 for directions on satin stitch appliqué.) The strawberry leaves and blossom were created using invisible appliqué. Since I only attached the leaves at the top and the blossom in the center, invisible appliqué allowed me to add depth and dimension to this banner: The invisible appliquéd pieces stick out from the banner slightly to give a three-dimensional quality. You can also use invisible appliqué to attach your strawberry, just adapt the directions below.

Selecting Fabrics and Threads

I chose the fabrics for this banner carefully. For the berries, I wanted a red print that resembled the surface of a strawberry. Strawberries are somewhat rough in texture, with small yellow seeds all over the surface. I loved the print I used the moment I saw it. I knew the green fabric for the leaves had to be either a solid or a very small print, but the solid green was just too boring. I chose a small floral print instead, a blue-green rather than a yellow-green, because it blends well with red.

For the background, I wanted to use an off-white or cream colored fabric to create an aged look. But when I realized that my strawberry blossom needed to be white, I was afraid that the background would look discolored or dirty beside the white blossom. That is why I selected a white-on-cream print with a very small meandering print that resembles stipple quilting. I was thrilled with the results of my fabric selection, but don't be limited by my choices: There are thousands of possibilities and combinations, so be creative.

The serger appliqué was done with black rayon thread in the upper (over) looper of the serger. The invisible appliqué was done with .004 mm nylon monofilament thread. I chose dark green pearl cotton, size #8, for the writing done with the cording foot.

Constructing the Background

1. Decide on a background size, then select fabric for the background and backing, as well as filling. I decided that 30 by 72 inches (approximately) would be a good size for my banner. I bought 2 yards of the white-on-cream background fabric along with 2 yards of unbleached muslin for the backing.

Because I wanted a quilted look, I decided to use polyester fleece between the background fabric and the backing.

2. Layer all three fabrics on a cutting mat, with the background and backing fabrics right sides together and the fleece on the bottom. Trim them to 30 by 72 inches with a rotary cutter and plastic ruler designed for rotary cutting. (See Fig. 5.1.) Set this "sandwich" of fabric aside without disturbing it.

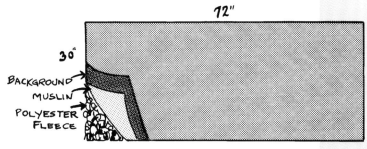

TRIM ON MAT & USE ROTARY CUTTER & RULER

Figure 5.1

3. To make the loops for the top of the banner I used the scrap of background fabric that was left over. I simply cut five 10- by- 10-inch squares, folded each one in half with right sides together, and stitched a ½-inch seam. Then I turned each one right side out and pressed it flat, with the seam centered on the back of the loop. Don't worry if the seam is pressed open or to one side. (See Fig. 5.2.) Then take each fabric tube and fold it in half, meeting the raw edges, forming a loop. (See Fig. 5.3.)

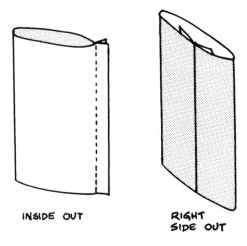

INSIDE OUT   RIGHT SIDE OUT

FABRIC TUBES

Figure 5.2

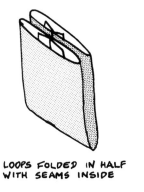

LOOPS FOLDED IN HALF
WITH SEAMS INSIDE

Figure 5.3

4. To position the five banner loops, simply place each loop between the background fabric and backing fabric with the raw edges of the loops even with the raw edges of the other fabrics. Space the loops at even intervals across the top of the banner. (See Fig. 5.4.) When you are satisfied with the loop placement, pin them into place.

5. Once you've pinned your loops in place, continue to pin all the way around your sandwich of fabric. Then with the fleece side down, stitch or serge all four sides with a 1/4- to 1/2-inch seam allowance. Leave a space open near the middle of the bottom to turn your banner right side out. (See Fig. 5.5.) Trim seams closely, especially corners, so they will turn easily and squarely. (See Fig. 5.6.) Stitch the bottom opening closed by hand after you are satisfied with the background.

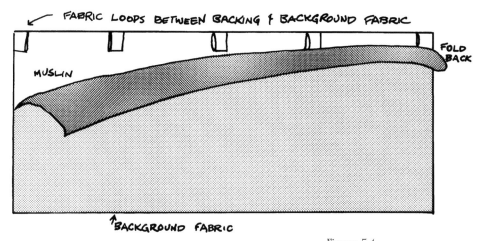

FABRIC LOOPS BETWEEN BACKING & BACKGROUND FABRIC

MUSLIN

FOLD BACK

BACKGROUND FABRIC

Figure 5.4

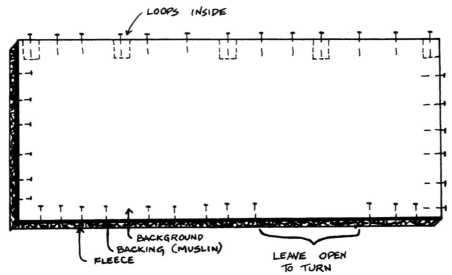

Figure 5.5

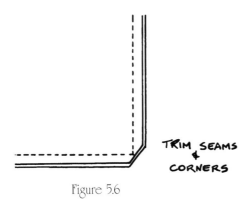

Figure 5.6

Appliquéing the Banner

Once you've prepared your backing and selected your appliqué fabrics, threads, and trims, you're ready to create your banner. You'll find the pattern for this banner in "Patterns" on page 92, along with directions for enlarging it to the size you need to follow the directions given here.

1. To trace your strawberries, put your pattern right side up on your light table. Place your red fabric for the strawberry right side up over the pattern so you can see your design through the fabric. Trace the strawberries onto the red fabric with a chalk pencil. Trace the large strawberry entirely, beginning and ending at the same point. Because the small strawberry will be tucked under the larger one, trace only from the two points where it meets the large strawberry, adding approximately 1/2 inch to tuck under the large strawberry.

2. Trace the strawberry stems onto the green fabric in exactly the same manner as you traced the strawberries.

3. Sew a rolled hem on your serger around the outside edges of the strawberries. Don't stitch any areas on the small strawberry that will be tucked under the larger one, because the rolled hem stitching may show through. Instead, allow a small amount of fabric, approximately 1/2 inch, to extend past the points where you started and stopped serging. This gives you

55

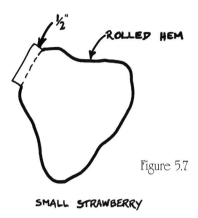

Figure 5.7

SMALL STRAWBERRY

a "tab" of fabric, as shown in Figure 5.7, to tuck under the large strawberry. See "Serger Appliqué" on page 35 for more on this technique.

4. With your serger, sew a rolled hem along the long edges of the strawberry stems. Leave a ¹/₂-inch tab on either end so you can tuck the stems under the other design pieces. (See Fig. 5.8.)

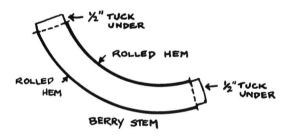

Figure 5.8

5. Next trace the leaves, which will be cut from the green fabric. Since the leaves are sewn using invisible appliqué, you need to reverse the pattern by placing the pattern over a light source and laying the green fabric over the leaves with the right side of the fabric down. Then trace each leaf with a chalk pencil that is easily visible on the green fabric. Allow enough extra fabric on the top of the blossom leaf so it can be tucked under the center of the blossom. (Since the blossom isn't sewn down around the edges, you want to finish the blossom leaf all the way under the blossom; the tab will fit under the center.)

6. After all the leaves are traced, you're ready to sew them using invisible appliqué. Make a sandwich with two layers of green fabric and the fleece that was left over from the background, with the fleece on the bottom and the green fabric right sides together. Now you can see the traced lines that will become your stitching lines. (See Fig. 5.9.) Stitch around the leaves entirely with a very short stitch length. Because the leaf will be bulky, you will be trimming your

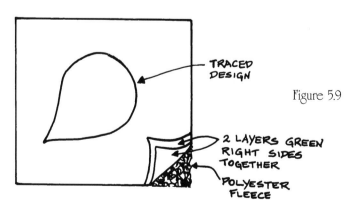

Figure 5.9

TRIMMING & SNIPPING

Figure 5.10

seam allowance to approximately ⅛ inch. A short stitch will hold much better on a narrow seam allowance. Snip into the seam allowance, just up to the stitching line, on curves and inside corners. Be careful not to cut the stitching! (See Fig. 5.10.) On the outside corners trim as close to the seam as possible, approximately ¹⁄₁₆ inch, to eliminate bulk.

7. The next step is to turn your leaves inside out. Simply snip an opening in the top layer of green fabric (the layer you traced on). Be careful to separate the layers of green fabric completely. You don't want to snip through both layers. Make it large enough to turn each leaf comfortably, but not larger than necessary. Turn each leaf right-side-out so it is no longer reversed and matches the pattern exactly. Use a long, thin object through the hole that you cut in the back of the leaf to gently push the points of the leaves into place. Make sure the object you are using is thin but blunt. (See Fig. 5.11.) A sharp tool will poke a hole in your fabric. There are various point-turning tools on the market.

Check at your local sewing supply store or see "Sources of Supplies" on page 91. When the leaves are all

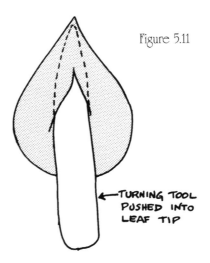

Figure 5.11

← TURNING TOOL PUSHED INTO LEAF TIP

turned, you can close the slits on the backside by hand.

8. Trace and sew the blossom the same way you sewed the leaves, using invisible appliqué. Then trace, stitch, snip, and turn the center of the blossom just like the leaves and the blossom, only this time don't use any fleece: All you need is two layers of fabric.

9. Using your pattern as a guide, pin your completed pieces into place, starting with the large strawberry. Next pin the small strawberry, tucking it under the large one. The small berry stem would be next, going from the large berry to the small one. Once they are pinned in place, topstitch them down. I used a piping foot especially designed for my sewing machine. The rolled hem fit in a groove under the foot and guided my stitching so that I was able to stitch right up next to the rolled hem. (See Fig. 5.12.) If you do not have a piping foot, you can use a zipper foot to stitch close to the rolled hem.

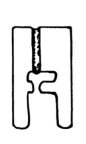

PIPING FOOT
BOTTOM

Figure 5.12

10. After these pieces are stitched down, pin on the long stem, the berry leaves and the blossom leaf. Then use invisible thread to stitch on the top of the leaves only. This creates a three-dimensional effect. I used a blind-hem stitch that was very narrow. You may also use a narrow zigzag.

11. To attach the blossom, pin the center and the blossom at the same time, making sure that you cover the back end of the blossom leaf. Then stitch around the yellow center with invisible thread, using the same stitch setting you used on the leaves. When you are pinning these pieces down, use lots of pins. Pin all the way through all of the layers—including the background. Try to avoid shifting of layers as much as possible. The reason I did all of my appliqué work after I sandwiched my background is because I wanted that slightly puckered, quilted look without quilting.

Lettering Your Banner

Now you can start the writing portion of your design. Trace your letters onto a sewable fusible, such as Heat 'n' Bond Lite or Wonder-Under, and press the fusible to the wrong side of the letter fabric. Cut them out, press them into place, and appliqué. Remember to reverse all of your letters when tracing them on the paper backing of the fusible.

If you chose to create your own lettering with cording or pearl cotton as I did, you will need to write or draw your letters on the background. You may use a disappearing, wash-out, or chalk marker. Stay away from markers that are permanent.

The writing on this banner was done with a special machine foot called a 7-Hole Cord Foot. (See Fig. 5.13.) It comes with a needle threader

7-HOLE
CORDING FOOT
Figure 5.13

to help you thread up to seven cords through the holes on the foot. Once it is threaded, you can then couch over these cords with any decorative or zig-zag stitch. Simply follow the lines you have drawn on the fabric and sew the cords into place.

Make sure the cording you have cut will be long enough to finish the job you started. The foot automatically places each cord down beside the next. It produces a flat braid effect. You can, of course, use a purchased braid or thick cording to couch over. Or simply satin stitch your letters. Another alternative would be to cut letters from fabric, and appliqué them into place. It's your banner; have fun with it!

Chapter 6

Angel Banner

A resplendent angel like this one called for elegant fabrics. This banner was sewn with brocade, satin, and tissue lamé. Transparent sparkle cloth gives her wings a soft, feathery feel. Michele Shepler designed this banner, which was sewn by author Ruth Ann Lowery.

Indoor Banner

Technique:

Appliqué with Free Motion Quilting

Finished Size:

36 by 45 inches

Although probably the most challenging project in this book, this elegant angel is also the most enjoyable to make. She would be a beautiful addition to any church or Christmas decorating scheme. A guardian angel is also a nice idea in a nursery, hospital, or nursing home. If you like, you can also adapt this pattern to make a reversible outdoor banner: Just follow the same techniques used on the Baby Carriage Banner on page 85. Before you begin sewing, I recommend you read all the instructions. You may also want to review the general appliqué techniques described in Chapter 3 on page 25 before you begin.

Above all, this is a creative project. As you select your fabrics and get ready to appliqué them, keep in mind that I am discussing the fabrics I used with the preparation techniques that worked for me. You may have to adapt these instructions to suit the fabrics you choose.

Fabric and Supplies:

Fabric requirements are given in yardage first. The measurements in parentheses are the actual dimensions needed. This will make it easy to use scraps of fabric you have at home.

1 yard 45-inch-wide royal blue satin for background

$7/8$ yard white brocade for dress and wings (30 × 30 inches)

$1/2$ yard sheer white for wing overlay (18 × 18 inches)

$1/2$ yard print for ribbons (20 × 20 inches)

$1/8$ yard flesh color for face and arms (6 × 10 inches)

$1/4$ yard brown Ultrasuede for hair (8 × 10 inches)

$1/8$ yard gold for horn (6" × 6")

1 yard polyester fleece

1 yard muslin for lining/backing

$1/2$ yard sequins for halo

Appliqué threads: Lamé for contrast, and matching cotton or polyester

Monofilament nylon thread .004 mm

Fusible thread

Sewable fusible

Stabilizer of your choice, if needed

Getting Started

Before you sew a stitch, you need to decide what size your banner will be, and then select your fabrics. The directions below are for a 36- by 45-inch banner. If you want your banner to be larger or smaller, you'll need to adjust the directions accordingly. You'll find the pattern for this banner in "Patterns" on page 92, along with directions for enlarging it to the size you need to follow the directions given here.

I started out with 1 yard of 45-inch-wide satin and used it sideways with the selvages on the top and bottom. If you adjust the size of the banner, be sure to size the background fabric so the entire angel fits on it comfortably. Keep in mind that even though no background fabric shows below the angel, you will need background fabric there initially.

Selecting Fabrics and Threads

A formal project calls for elegant fabrics, and this angel banner was no exception. She was sewn using brocade, satin, tissue lamé, and Ultrasuede. Lamé threads and sequins add to the luxurious effect.

The first step in any project is to create it in your mind's eye. Think of the message you are trying to convey, and try to imagine what colors and textures will look the best. For this project, I wanted rich-looking, reflective fabrics and threads. I knew that the background for this banner needed to be a blue sky. I started with that color and fabric first. I wanted a bright, royal blue. Since I wanted the sky to be colorful but plain, a patterned fabric like brocade wasn't suitable. Lamés were too flashy. The baroque satin was exactly what I was searching for, because it has a beautiful sheen but doesn't overpower the angel.

White was the only color I ever considered for the angel's dress and wings. Since I wanted a very dressy fabric, I choose a brocade that has a pearlized thread running through it that catches the light from any angle. The fabric overlay I used for the wings is a transparent sparkle cloth. It has a pearlized appearance and is a great companion for the brocade.

The angel's hair is created from a piece of chocolate brown Ultrasuede, a choice I agonized over. I wanted something that looked like hair, but fake fur wasn't formal enough and velvet is too difficult to use for appliqué. Ultrasuede, which is easy to appliqué with, has a soft, nappy texture that was just right. Small specialty sewing shops, where I found the Ultrasuede I used, often cut it up into appliqué-sized pieces. This way you can purchase many different colors for a reasonable price.

The angel's ribbons and face and hands were created with two of my favorite fabrics: Calico and muslin. For her face, I tea-dyed the muslin to get the shade I wanted for her skin.

To tea-dye muslin, place about six tea bags into very hot water (about 1½ quarts) and let them steep for awhile. Then hand dip your fabric in and out of the tea water until you have reached the color intensity you want. Once the fabric has dried it is ready to be used. The Angel's ribbons are a beautiful pansy print with gold accents that I fell in love with the minute I saw it.

The horn was created by fusing tissue lamé to muslin. Fusing the lamé stabilizes it and keeps it from fraying. Another method of stabilizing lamé is pressing a fusible tricot interfacing to the wrong side of the lamé. I use this method when sewing garments or adding lamé to a quilt. But for appliqué I like the extra stabilization and strength that the muslin backing adds.

The accents were sewn with a variety of lamé threads. I chose a pearlized white lamé thread to appliqué the dress and wings, because I wanted the stitching to blend with the design. It complemented the brocade and sparkle cloth perfectly. (You could use a contrasting thread to appliqué, if you wish.) The accent stitching on the dress, wings, and horn was sewn with metallic gold lamé thread. I also used it to appliqué the ribbons on my angel, because it brought out the gold accents in my calico. I chose the gold lamé not only for its reflective quality, but also for its cooperative nature: Lamé threads are much easier to sew with than the metallic threads used in the past.

The old metallics tend to shred and bunch when conditions are not perfect. The new lamé threads, which are a solid strand of tinsel-like material, sew beautifully with an ordinary 80/12 needle. All you need to do is lower the upper tension slightly. The manufacturers have all the instructions available for you when you purchase these threads.

The muslin face and hands were stitched with a standard polyester thread. Since I wanted thread and stitching that would blend with the fabric, not stand out, I used a shaded appliqué stitch on this part of the project. It avoids the sharp lines of normal satin stitched appliqué. See "Shaded Appliqué" on page 35 for more on this technique.

Sequins seemed to be the only choice for a halo. I tried to select a gold fabric to appliqué in a semi-circle behind the angel's head, but everything I tried was wrong. When I was almost at my wit's end, I decided to try showing just the edge of the halo with a gold braid. Somehow it seemed too insignificant. This angel worked hard for her halo, and she deserved a fancy one! The sequin trim I found was just right, fancy enough, not overwhelming.

Preparing Your Fabrics

Many of the fabrics I chose for this project could be a problem to appliqué. Fabrics that fray, are very thin, or will be slippery against the background fabric will need to be fused before you begin. Since I wanted the design pieces on this banner to look soft, almost three-dimensional, I did not fuse them to the background fabric. (The satin background fabric doesn't hold on to a fusible very well anyway.) Instead, I fused some of the appliqué pieces to muslin independently. Muslin is lightweight, yet stable. It has a nice, tight weave, but adds little weight and bulk. I fused the brocade for the dress and wings (all one piece), the lamé for the horn, and the tea-dyed muslin for the face and hands. I did not fuse the Ultrasuede hair, the calico ribbons, or the transparent fabric overlay for the wings to muslin.

To prepare your fabrics that need to be fused to muslin, trace those pattern pieces onto a sewable fusible. When tracing the dress and wings, trace the wings as though they are really behind the angel's head. Putting the hair over the wings will be easier than trying to fit the hair next to the wing. (See Fig. 6.1.)

Because you will be fusing the product to a muslin backing, you can trace directly from the pattern and the design will face the right direction when it's finished. Fuse the product to the muslin, following the manufacturer's instructions. Then cut out the design pieces, and peel the paper from the fusible.

Next, press the cut-out muslin shapes into place on the wrong side of the fabric you have chosen for each piece—the brocade for the dress or the lamé for the horn, for example. To do this, place your appliqué fabric wrong side up and put the muslin on top with the fusible side down against the wrong side of your appliqué fabric. Then fuse the muslin to the back of the appliqué fabric, let it cool, and cut the design out, using the muslin shape as the guide. (See Fig. 6.2.)

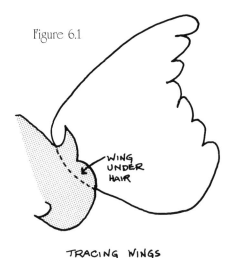

Figure 6.1

TRACING WINGS

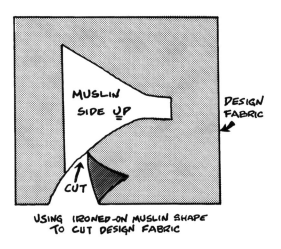

USING IRONED-ON MUSLIN SHAPE TO CUT DESIGN FABRIC

Figure 6.2

Now you can prepare the design pieces that don't need to be fused to muslin—the Ultrasuede hair, calico ribbons, and wing overlay fabric. The easiest way to get the Ultrasuede hair design piece ready is to turn the pattern piece over on a light table and trace the hair shape onto a fusible product. Then fuse the product to the wrong side of the Ultrasuede and cut it out. That way, you can fuse the hair into place before you sew.

To trace the ribbons, lay the pattern right side up on a light table. Lay the ribbon fabric, also right side up, over the pattern. Trace the ribbons entirely. They will all be cut and sewn on in one piece, except the piece behind her wing, which you need to trace separately. (See Fig. 6.3.) Then, with a fusible thread in the bobbin, stitch on all lines of the ribbons. Use an elongated stitch and slightly tightened upper tension. Cut out the ribbons a scant ⅛ inch outside of the stitching lines. (See Fig. 6.4.)

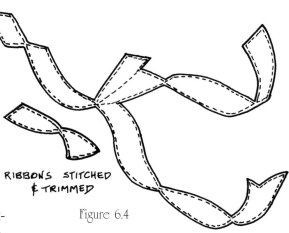

RIBBONS STITCHED & TRIMMED

Figure 6.4

Finally, trace the wing design onto the sheer wing overlay fabric using a marker that can be easily removed. Just as you did when you traced the dress and wings, trace the wings as though they go behind the angel's head in order to eliminate fitting problems in the head area. It is much easier to appliqué the hair over the wings.

Sewing the Dress and Wings

Now that all of your fabrics are prepared, you can begin to appliqué the dress and wings, which are the pieces "farthest back" in the banner. Everything else is placed on top of them. Follow the steps below to get them in position:

1. Carefully pin the dress part of the design piece into place on the background fabric. Space pins about every inch. Make sure you have room to fit all the pieces onto the background; it's easy to forget to allow enough room for the horn. (See Fig. 6.5.)

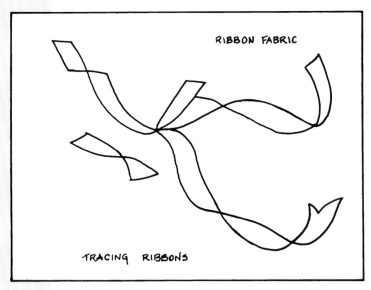

RIBBON FABRIC

TRACING RIBBONS

Figure 6.3

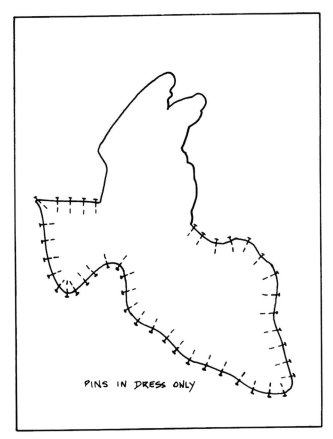

PINS IN DRESS ONLY

Figure 6.5

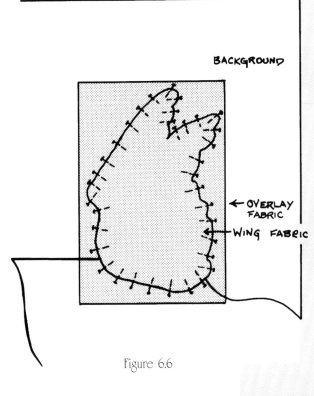

BACKGROUND

← OVERLAY FABRIC

← WING FABRIC

Figure 6.6

2. Once the dress and wings are in place, lay the sheer wing overlay over the wing section. (You will be able to see through the overlay.) Line up the traced wings on the overlay fabric with the edges of the wing fabric already in place. Then pin through all of the layers—background, wing, and wing overlay. As before, space pins about every inch. (See Fig. 6.6) Pinning every inch may seem excessive, but it saves time in the long run. If your appliqué shifts while you are satin stitching, you will have to pick out all those stitches, and start again. The line on the overlay fabric becomes your stitching line. It should be exactly the same, or at least very close, to the edge of the wing fabric underneath. If they aren't the same, use the edge of the wing fabric as your stitching guide. (See Fig. 6.7.)

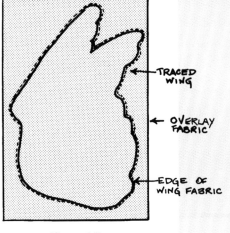

TRACED WING

← OVERLAY FABRIC

EDGE OF WING FABRIC

Figure 6.7

3. The wings need to be straight-stitched into place before they are appliquéd. To do this, set your machine for a straight stitch, normal stitch length, and lighten the pressure on your presser foot. This will help you to maneuver around curves and corners. The

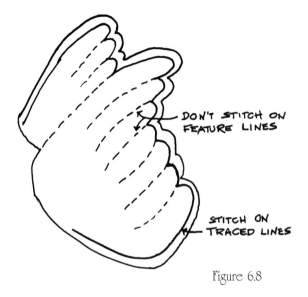

DON'T STITCH ON FEATURE LINES

STITCH ON TRACED LINES

Figure 6.8

lightened pressure also helps keep the multiple layers of fabric from shifting. If you have one, you may also want to use a dual feeding foot or a walking foot for your machine. I always put the walking foot on my sewing machine anytime I think I may have a problem with shifting layers of fabric. Stitch through all three layers, using the edge of the wings as your guide. Don't stitch the feature lines at this point. (See Fig. 6.8.) Remove each pin as you approach it. Don't try to sew over pins with your machine. Striking a pin can bring your project to a abrupt halt. You can cause your machine timing to go off, scratch the hook, or break an internal part that may be very expensive to replace.

4. Once you've stitched the wings into place, trim away any excess overlay fabric. Leave about $1/16$ to $1/8$ inch of fabric outside of the stitching line. If you cut too close, the overlay fabric may ravel

and pull away. If you leave too much fabric, on the other hand, the satin appliqué stitch you sew on in Step 5 may not cover the edge of the leftover overlay fabric and the line of straight stitching you just completed. Appliqué scissors are wonderful for trimming areas like this, because they allow you to trim very close with great accuracy.

5. Next, thread your machine with the lamé thread you selected to appliqué this part of the project. (I used a pearlized white lamé.) Thread the bobbin with ordinary white polyester thread or inexpensive basting thread, both of which are cheaper than the lamé. Be sure that your upper tension is set low enough that the bobbin threads don't show on top. Then stitch the feature lines on the wings to give your angel's feathers definition.

6. Now, you can begin to appliqué. Since the fabrics I chose created a firm base for appliqué, I didn't need to add any type of stabilizer. If you think that you need to stabilize your design, do so. Pin tearaway or heat-away stabilizers that come in a sheet, onto the back of your background fabric, through all layers of the design. You don't want the stabilizer shifting as you sew. With the lamé thread still in your machine, set your machine for a satin appliqué stitch that is wide enough to cover the straight stitching line and the raw edge of the wings. (See Fig. 6.9.) Make the stitch length short enough to create a tight, satiny stitch. You will sew

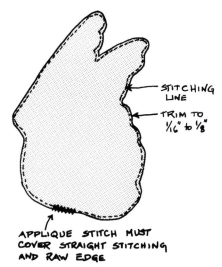

STITCHING LINE

TRIM TO 1/16" to 1/8"

APPLIQUE STITCH MUST COVER STRAIGHT STITCHING AND RAW EDGE

Figure 6.9

Adding the Details

The ribbon, horn, face, and hands will give your emerging angel the personality she needs. Here's how to apply them:

1. After the wings and dress are finished, position the ribbons and fuse them into place. See "Position and Fuse the Design" on page 42 for directions on fusing with fusible thread. Remember to fuse the piece of ribbon that is next to the wings. (See Fig. 6.11.)

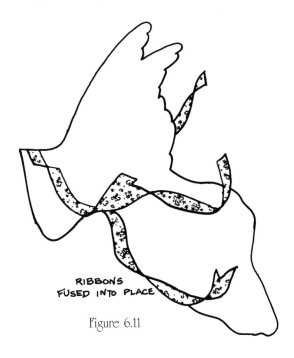

RIBBONS FUSED INTO PLACE

Figure 6.11

over this area only once, so you want good stitch coverage. Start to appliqué somewhere on the wings so you can adjust the width of the stitch properly. Begin in an area that is straight and easy, so you have a chance to get the feel of the stitching before you have to maneuver around a curve or corner. (See Fig. 6.10.) Go around the wings entirely, pivoting on curves, and turning corners according to the instructions in "Mastering Corners and Curves" on page 30. When the wings are done, continue around the dress following the same instructions.

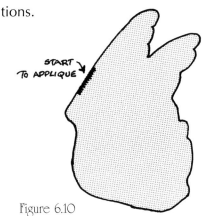

START TO APPLIQUE

Figure 6.10

2. After the ribbons are fused into place, you can appliqué them. First decide if you need to stabilize the fabric. The ribbons that are on the dress may not need stabilization before you appliqué, but the piece of ribbon next to the wings will. Thread your machine with metallic gold lamé thread. As you did for the white lamé thread for the

wings and dress, you can thread the bobbin with ordinary white polyester thread or inexpensive basting thread. Again, be sure that your upper tension is set low enough that the bobbin threads don't show on top. Satin stitch the ribbons into place as you did the wings and dress.

3. Sew the accent stitching onto the wings and dress with the same gold thread. I sewed the accent lines on the dress with a narrow satin stitch. I used a 3-step straight stitch for the accent stitching on the wings. This stitch is also called the reinforced stretch stitch. The needle stitches over each stitch three times. This stitch is great for any type of topstitching. Each stitch is bold and visible. I think it looks best when used with a slightly longer stitch length than normal.

4. The angel's hands, face, hair, and horn all have to fit together. I lightly pinned all of these pieces in place before I started to sew anything. First decide where the hands should be in relationship to the sleeves. (See Fig. 6.12.) Then place the horn pieces in the hands. Put the bell of the horn out in front of the hands (See Fig. 6.13.) and the mouthpiece behind the hands. Tuck the ends of the horn pieces just slightly under the hands. Once the hands and horn are in place, you can position the face and hair: They should line up with the angel's sleeve, wings, and horn. When you are satisfied that the angel looks as she should, pin everything into place. Use lots of pins to prevent

PLACING ARMPIECE WITH SLEEVE

Figure 6.12

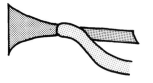

PLACING HORN IN HAND

Figure 6.13

shifting. If you are fusing any of your pieces into place, now is the time to do it.

5. Appliqué the horn first, but stabilize the area first. I appliquéd the angel's horn with the gold lamé thread that I used on the ribbons. Start at one side of the angel's hand, and appliqué down one side, around the bell of the horn, and back up the other side to meet her hand again. Then appliqué the two long sides of the mouthpiece end of the horn.

6. The hands and face are appliquéd next. I used a polyester thread that matched my muslin exactly, because I didn't want the appliqué stitching on the hands to stand out. I also selected a shaded appliqué stitch because I thought that, even though the thread matched perfectly, a normal satin

stitch appliqué would create a ridged effect on a plain, smooth fabric like muslin. See "Shaded Stitch Appliqué" on page 35 for more on this technique.

7. The last piece to be appliquéd is the hair. Because Ultrasuede doesn't ravel, it can be attached with an heirloom appliqué stitch, sometimes called a blanket or buttonhole stitch. Heirloom appliqué stitch is sewn with the needle beginning just off the edge of the appliqué piece, dropping into the background fabric. After a few stitches are sewn into the background fabric at the edge of the appliqué piece, the needle swings onto the appliqué piece for just one stitch. Then the needle returns to the edge of the appliqué piece and starts all over. (See Fig. 6.14.) This stitch gives a light, handsewn look to your appliqué, but does not sew the edge of the appliqué piece in a solid manner that would stop raveling. Therefore you must either fuse the design if you are using a fabric that ravels, or use a material that does not ravel, like felt or Ultrasuede. If you chose to use this stitch on a fabric that ravels, and you don't want to fuse the design first, you will need to turn the outside edges under. Most

HEIRLOOM APPLIQUE STITCH

Figure 6.14

quilters turn their edges under 1/8 to 1/4 inch. Then you will be stitching on a turned edge rather than a raw edge.

Finishing the Banner

Now your angel is appliquéd and you are ready to finished your banner. When I designed this project, I wanted the edge of the banner to follow the shape of the angel's dress, sleeve, and horn. After much consideration and many sleepless nights, I decided to appliqué her to the blue satin and just make the banner rectangular. It would be all right if the blue sky showed below her dress . . . after all she is flying! So I must confess, this is exactly what I started to do, but when I turned the angel over to the back side and saw all the white bobbin thread I had used, I realized just how I could make the banner follow her shape. If you turn your banner over, and follow the directions below, you'll see the secret, too:

1. When you look at the back of your banner, you'll see the shape of your entire angel stitched out. The line along the edges where you appliquéd her dress, sleeve, and horn become your guidelines for stitching on a backing for your ban-

ner. Draw a line straight up from the back of her dress and from the horn to form the side edges of the banner. (See Fig. 6.15.) Be sure to position the selvages at top and bottom.

2. Cut pieces of polyester fleece and lining fabric (I chose muslin) that will be large enough to cover the entire angel and the sky between the lines you drew. Don't be skimpy with the lining and fleece. It is better to trim some away, than to cut yourself short.

3. Layer the three fabrics. First place the fleece down on the table. Lay the lining fabric on top with the right side up. Finally, lay the angel facing down on the lining fabric. Align all the pieces so you will be stitching through all three layers at all times. Then pin all three layers securely, with pins at 1- to 1½-inch intervals apart all the way around the stitching lines. (The stitching lines are the vertical lines you traced and the outline of the dress, sleeve, and horn on the bottom edge of the angel. (See Fig. 6.16)

4. Thread your machine with a normal polyester or cotton sewing thread, and set it for a very short straight stitch. You will be trimming your seam allowance to only ⅛ inch, so you will want a stitch that is going to hold when the banner is turned right-side out. Using your appliqué stitching as your guide, sew a seam just outside the appliqué stitching line. Remember to remove the pins as you stitch up to them. (The distance between the

Figure 6.15

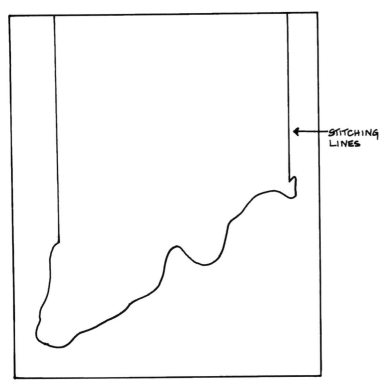

Figure 6.16

two stitching lines, as shown in Figure 6.17, is probably only $1/32$ inch.) To help keep the fabric layers from shifting as I stitched, I used the walking foot on my machine. When you are beginning and ending at the top edge of the banner, don't backstitch. You will be removing a few of these stitches later when you sew your casing, and backstitching only makes this task more difficult.

Figure 6.17

5. When you have stitched around the angel entirely, trim

the seam allowance to approximately $1/8$ inch. Take your time, and don't snip into your stitching line. It is better to leave too much and trim again later than to cut too much the first time. You may also need to snip into the seam allowance in areas where there are sharp curves, to allow the banner to turn properly. The corners on the horn need to be trimmed very closely so they will turn into a sharp point. Once you've trimmed the seams, turn the banner. If you sandwiched the fabrics properly, you should have the angel on the front, the lining on the back, and the fleece layered in between. If any areas pucker or pull when you turn them, go to those areas on the inside of the banner, and make very small snips into the seam allowance. Be careful! I found that I only had to make a few snips. A $1/8$-inch seam usually turns very well.

6. Take your angel to the ironing board and press the outside edges of the banner so they will lay flat. Then turn your banner over and press from the lining side. (The formal fabrics on the front may melt if the iron is too hot; lamé threads also are sensitive to heat.) If you lined your banner with muslin, as I did, it will take a lot of heat and press nice

and flat, with no puckers or pulled areas. As you press, coax the muslin to the back so the lining does not show from the front.

Quilting the Angel

As beautiful as she is, your angel needs some definition, depth, and personality. She needs to stand out from the background, not blend into it. I think the best way to add depth and definition is to outline-quilt the design. Outline quilting will also tie all the layers together and add texture and substance to the banner.

Since you will be quilting from one area to the next, going from one color of fabric to another, invisible monofilament nylon thread is the only choice for this task. Otherwise, you would have to change thread color every time you move to a new design piece. Invisible thread is forgiving because it is, as the name implies, invisible. If you don't stitch exactly where you intended to, the thread won't scream your mistake out at you. Be sure to buy .004 mm nylon thread. It is as fine as a hair on your head and very easy to work

with. You will recognize it because it comes on a small cone, not a spool like the coarser ones. The only thing you need to be aware of is that if you overfill a plastic bobbin with monofilament nylon thread, it could break. Because this thread is so fine, even a half-filled bobbin lasts a very long time. So I only fill my plastic bobbins about half full to be safe.

Baste the layers of your banner together before you start quilting. You can do this by hand using either a running stitch or a padding stitch. (See Fig. 6.18.) The running stitch, as the name implies, just runs straight down the fabric. Put the needle in through all three layers, going straight ahead, and coming up through again. The padding stitch is a little easier to accomplish because you can stitch left to right or right to left through all three layers, come up out of the top layer, pull the needle and thread toward you, and stitch again from side to side. This method of basting seems to go faster. If you wish, you can baste your banner with safety pins. I think this takes longer to do initially: They are difficult to stitch over, and they take

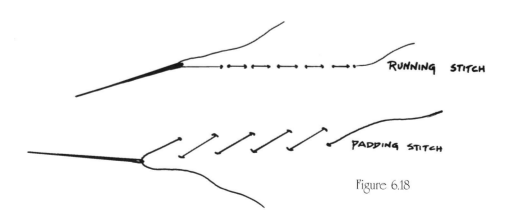

Figure 6.18

longer to remove than the basting stitching. Safety pins also leave larger holes in the fabric.

Once you've basted, you are ready to quilt. For directions, see "Free-Motion Quilting" on page 21.

Sewing the Casing

The last step is to finish the casing at the top of the banner. Decide how your banner will be hung and plan your casing accordingly. It will need to be large enough to fit over the pole you have chosen. When you have decided how wide the casing should be, you can prepare the fleece and lining accordingly.

The fleece and lining you cut to fit the background will have to be trimmed now. If you had cut them to the exact size when you sandwiched your layers, by the time you stitched, turned, and quilted, the layers may have shifted or pulled and become too short. This is why I told you not to backstitch at the top edge of the banner when you were stitching the sides.

If you need a 2-inch casing for your pole, then the fabric included in the casing area is actually 4 inches. To make the casing, you will turn down 2 inches and topstitch it. (See Fig. 6.19.) Therefore the lining fabric

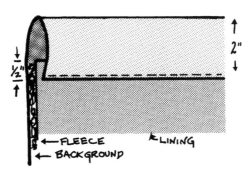

Figure 6.19

and the fleece should be trimmed so that only about $1/2$" will be stitched up into the casing.

To create your casing, simply fold over the amount of fabric you need and topstitch along the open edge. If you need to turn under the edge to finish it, you can turn under approximately $1/4$ inch and then topstitch. If the selvage is the top edge of the background fabric you don't need to turn any fabric under. If you have made your banner of washable fabrics, you may wish to trim the selvage off first. Some selvages shrink when washed. My angel will be drycleaned, so I wasn't worried about the selvages shrinking.

Now your angel is finished. Be sure to hang her from a pole or rod that is pretty or decorative—she deserves it!

Chapter 7

Halloween Banner

Decorate for a Halloween party with this colorful banner. Or just celebrate ghosts, goblins and things that go bump in the night. This banner was designed and sewn by author Ruth Ann Lowery.

Outdoor Banner

Technique:

Reversible Applique

Finished Size:

30 by 45 inches

Fabric and Supplies:

Fabric requirements are given in yardage first. The measurements in parentheses are the actual dimensions needed. All the fabric used for this project is 200 denier nylon.

7/8 yard lilac for background (30 × 45 inches)

1/4 yard black for bats and eyes (9 × 15 inches)

3/8 yard white for ghost (12 × 16 inches)

3/8 yard orange for pumpkins (13 × 24 inches)

1/8 yard gold brown for stems (4 × 5 inches)

3/8 yard Spanish yellow for moon (13 × 13 inches)

Rayon thread, the colors of your choice

Fusible thread

Stabilizer of your choice

Leather banner tab

Chalk markers

Let this spooky Halloween ghost send shivers down the spines of trick-or-treaters who visit your house. Scary bats against a full moon and bright pumpkins are sure to please them all. Best of all, this is probably the easiest reversible outdoor banner project to make. It is a good first project, since the design is simple and it doesn't require any special hemming techniques.

Sewing Your Halloween Banner

You'll find brief directions for making the banner below. Read through them, and then turn to "Reversible Appliqué" on page 39, where you'll find complete and detailed directions for making reversible banners like this one. You can either cut all the pieces and appliqué them as described there, or if fitting all the pieces together at one time seems intimidating, you can sew the eyes on the ghost and the bat on the moon before you appliqué the ghost and moon to the background.

1. Size and square up the background fabric, then hem it and sew the casing. For complete directions, see "Hemming and Casing Construction" on page 17.

2. Prepare the design pieces. You'll find the pattern for this banner in "Patterns" on page 92, along with directions for enlarging it to the size you need to follow the directions given here.

3. Trace the design pieces onto the nylon fabric with a chalk marker.

4. Stitch on the exterior lines of each design piece with fusible thread in the bobbin. Thread the top of your machine with the color of rayon thread you will be using to appliqué that piece later.

5. Cut each design piece out. Stay a scant ⅛ inch outside the fusible thread stitching lines.

6. Using the paper pattern as a guide, pin all the design pieces into place on your hemmed-and-cased background fabric.

7. Fuse the design pieces onto the background. Set your iron for high heat with steam. Remember to use a pressing cloth, because nylon fabric melts.

8. Appliqué all the design pieces. Remember to stabilize the fabric before you sew. See Figure 7.1 for pointers on where to start and stop your appliqué stitching.

9. Carefully trim the background from behind the design.

10. Appliqué the design again, this time from the back side. You won't need to stabilize this time.

11. Stitch all accent or feature lines. Remember to stabilize the fabric first.

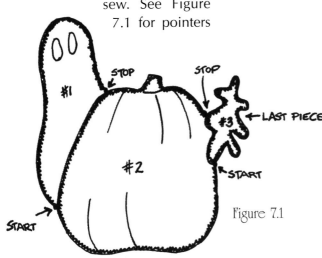

Figure 7.1

Sunflower Banner

"Plant" a bouquet of cheery sunflowers in front of your house with this brightly colored banner. It's a handsome design you'll enjoy year after year. Michele Shepler designed this banner, which was sewn by author Ruth Ann Lowery.

Outdoor Banner

Technique:

Reversible Appliqué

Finished Size:

30 by 45 inches

Fabric and Supplies:

Fabric requirements are given in yardage first. The measurements in parentheses are the actual dimensions, which will make it easy to use scraps of fabric you already have. All fabrics for this banner are 200 denier nylon.

⁷/₈ yard black for background (30 × 45 inches)

¹/₂ yard Spanish yellow for petals (20 × 30 inches)

¹/₄ yard gold-brown for flower centers (10 × 15 inches)

⁵/₈ yard Irish green for stems and leaves (21 × 20 inches)

Rayon thread, the colors of your choice

Fusible thread

Stabilizer of your choice

Leather banner tab

Chalk markers

What better way to greet summer than with this cheerful bouquet of sunflowers? Whether you hang it from your own front porch or give it to a friend, it will bring smiles to faces again and again. You'll find directions for making it below. There are two special techniques you'll learn when you make this banner: Keep them in mind as you read through the directions. First, I've provided some special techniques for piecing the flowers successfully. Secondly, note that the stems of the flowers extend into the hemmed section of the banner. That means you'll have to follow the background directions carefully: When designs are included in the hem, the banner is appliquéd first and hemmed last.

Piecing Your Sunflower

The golden petals of these sunflowers surround a brown center that is pieced into the center like a puzzle. (See Fig. 8.1.) Piecing the banner like a puzzle, by cutting out the center of each petal piece and piecing in the brown center does require more accuracy when you trace the pieces, stitch them with fusible thread, and then trim. I think the light, transparent look of the finished banner is worth it, though. If you place layers of colors, (like the brown centers on top of the yellow petals) without cutting out the centers it only makes stitching and trimming more difficult. It also yields a thick heavy look if you stitch multiple layers together.

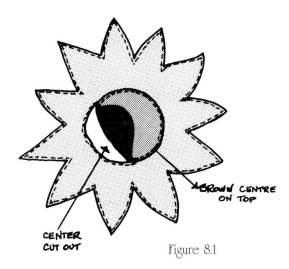

CENTER
CUT OUT

BROWN CENTRE
ON TOP

Figure 8.1

fusible thread in the bobbin, cutting them out, and fusing them to the background fabric. Both methods work equally well. Use the instructions that work best for you.

Sewing Your Sunflower Banner

Once you've read through the directions below, turn to "Reversible Appliqué" on page 39, where you'll find complete and detailed directions for making reversible banners like this one.

1. Size and square up the background fabric, but don't hem it yet.

2. Prepare the design pieces. You'll find the pattern for this banner in "Patterns" on page 92, along with directions for enlarging it to the size you need to follow the directions given here.

If you find that puzzle piecing is too difficult, don't worry, the more banners you make, the more accurate your tracing and stitching gets. In the meantime I have a method that builds one layer of the banner at a time and avoids piecing the design like a puzzle. This will also help you avoid stitching through multiple layers.

Trace the golden petals of the sunflowers. Then trace the gold-brown centers. Stitch with fusible thread in the bobbin on the traced lines of the brown centers only. Trim around the stitching lines on the centers, leaving a scant 1/8 inch. Don't stitch anything on the petals yet. Fuse the centers to the petals. (See Fig. 8.2.) Then stabilize the fabrics and satin stitch around the centers, appliquéing them to the petals. When you have finished, cut the back away. In this case, the background is the petal fabric. Now you can continue with the rest of the pieces as you would normally, stitching around the petals with

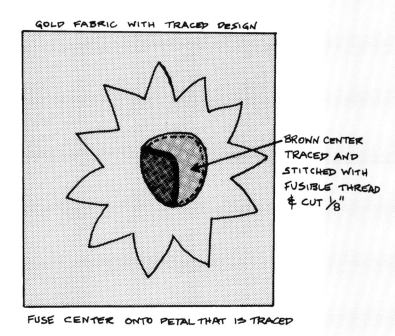

GOLD FABRIC WITH TRACED DESIGN

BROWN CENTER
TRACED AND
STITCHED WITH
FUSIBLE THREAD
& CUT 1/8"

FUSE CENTER ONTO PETAL THAT IS TRACED

Figure 8.2

3. Trace appliqué design pieces onto the nylon fabric with a chalk marker.

4. Stitch on the exterior lines of each design piece with fusible thread in the bobbin. Thread the top of your machine with the color of rayon thread you will be using to appliqué that piece later.

5. Cut each design piece out. Stay a scant 1/8" outside of the fusible thread stitching lines.

6. Using the paper pattern as a guide, pin all design pieces into place on the background fabric.

7. Fuse the design pieces onto the background. Set your iron for high heat with steam. Remember to use a pressing cloth, because nylon fabric melts.

8. Appliqué all design pieces. Remember to stabilize your fabric before you sew.

9. Carefully trim the background from behind the design.

10. Appliqué the design again, this time from the back side. You won't need to stabilize this time.

11. Stitch all accent or feature lines. Remember to stabilize first.

12. Hem the background and sew the casing. For complete directions, see "Hemming and Casing Construction" on page 17.

Baby Carriage Banner

Announce the arrival of your pride and joy with a Baby Carriage Banner. You can sew one with this color scheme, or design your own. This banner was designed and sewn by author Ruth Ann Lowery.

Outdoor Banner

Technique:

Reversible Appliqué

Finished Size:

30 by 45 inches

Fabric and Supplies:

Fabric requirements are given in yardage first. The measurements in parentheses are the actual dimensions needed. This will make it easy to use scraps of fabric you have at home. All the fabric for this banner is 200 denier nylon.

7/8 yard United Nations blue for background (30 × 45 inches)

3/4 yard crocus pink for carriage (27 × 27 inches)

1/4 yard white for blankets and wheels (18 × 24 inches)

3/8 yard black for tires and handle (13 × 26 inches)

Rayon thread, the colors of your choice

Fusible thread

Stabilizer of your choice

Leather banner tab

Chalk markers

What new parents don't want the world to know they have a new baby? Wouldn't this banner make a great baby shower gift? It's much more interesting than bibs, rattles, and bumper pads. You could make the banner and buy a banner pole. Then, as the child grows up you can give him or her a birthday banner, holiday banners, and even back-to-school banners. We even make banners of childrens' favorite cartoon characters. (Even though designs for cartoon characters are trademarks, and can't be sold, you can make one for a gift.)

This is one of my own designs. I have a dear friend and coworker, Michele Shepler, who does most of my designing, but since this is my book, I wanted to include a few designs of my own. I wanted a banner that would celebrate a birth, but I was tired of balloons, storks, and babies in diapers.

You'll learn two special techniques when you make this banner. First, I wanted to include a design that goes off the edge of the banner. The wheels of the carriage seemed to be the ideal place to teach this technique. Secondly, the blanket is actually three-dimensional—it hangs out of the carriage on both sides. I had a lot of fun with this banner, and I hope you will, too.

Getting Started

Once you've read through the directions below, turn to "Reversible Appliqué" on page 39, where you'll find complete and detailed directions for making reversible banners like this one.

The first step is to size and square up the background fabric, then hem it and sew the casing. For complete directions, see "Hemming and Casing Construction" on page 17. Then prepare the design pieces. You'll find the pattern for this banner in "Patterns" on page 92, along with directions for enlarging it to the size you need to follow the directions given here.

Finally, before you start assembling your banner, you need to trace all the design pieces onto the nylon fabric with a chalk marker. Trace the carriage as one piece, in this case on pink. The tires are traced on black and the wheels on white. When tracing the tires, be sure to trace the small marks that are approximately halfway down on each side. They mark the points where the tires leave the edge of the banner, and you'll need to know where they are later. (See Fig. 9.1.) The carriage handle is also traced onto black. For the carriage blanket to be three-dimensional and show on both sides, you will need to trace two blankets onto white. Keep in mind that these colors are suggestions only: Feel free to come up with your own combination of colors.

Constructing the Wheels

The tire and the wheel are stitched together just like the sunflower petals and centers in the

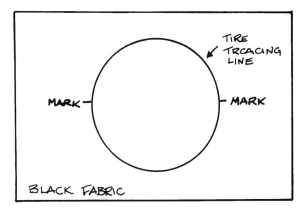

Figure 9.1

Sunflower Banner in Chapter 8. You'll find an illustration of this technique on page 83. Here's how to make them:

1. Stitch with fusible thread in your bobbin around the circumference of each wheel (the white fabric) Don't stitch with fusible thread on the hub of the wheel or the spokes.

2. Trim around the stitching lines, leaving a scant ⅛ inch. Then fuse each wheel to the center of the black circle you traced for the tire. The tires are traced only, not sewn or trimmed yet. (See Fig. 9.2.)

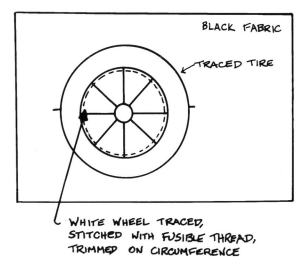

Figure 9.2

3. Stabilize the design and appliqué each wheel to the tire fabric.

4. Trim the black fabric away from the back of each white wheel. Then continue on with the design as though the tire and wheel are one piece. You can do the accent stitching (spokes and hub) on the wheels now or wait until the banner is assembled. In the same manner, you can satin stitch around the back of the wheels now or wait until you satin stitch around the rest of the back of the banner.

5. Next, stitch the top of each tire with the fusible thread in the bobbin, sewing from mark to mark. (See Fig. 9.3.) Then cut the tires out a scant ⅛ inch outside the stitching lines. Don't cut around the lines that haven't been sewn with fusible thread. Leave at least ½" to 1" of fabric outside of the traced lines. (See Fig. 9.4.)

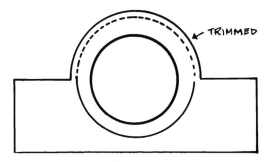

Figure 9.4

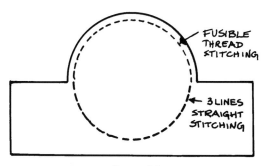

Figure 9.5

6. Put your appliqué thread in the bobbin of your machine, and set it for a short, straight stitch. Then stitch around the rest of the circumference of the tire three times, trying to keep your stitching lines right on top of each other. (See Fig. 9.5.) When you appliqué the banner, these straight stitching lines will hold the satin stitching, which eventually forms the bottom of your banner, in place. Don't appliqué the tires now, though: Put these pieces aside and finish preparing the other design pieces.

Sewing the Baby Blanket

The baby blanket pieces are made in almost the same way as the tires. Here's how:

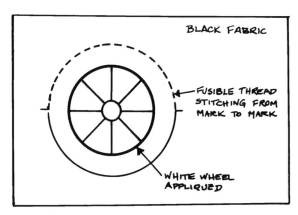

Figure 9.3

1. Stitch with fusible thread along the straight, top edge of both blankets. Trim the straight edge down to a scant ⅛ inch outside the stitching line. (See Fig. 9.6.)

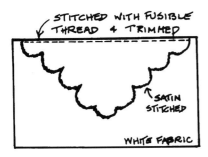

Figure 9.6

2. Put your appliqué thread in the bobbin of your machine. Set your machine for a short straight stitch, and stitch on the traced scalloped edges of each blanket. Stitch over these traced lines three times, as you did on the wheels, trying to keep your stitching lines right on top of each other.

3. Next, stabilize the fabric and do a close satin stitch on the scalloped portion of the blankets. (See Fig. 9.6.) Using appliqué scissors or small embroidery scissors, trim all around the scalloped, satin-stitched edges. Get as close as you can without nipping the satin stitch. Then put the blanket pieces aside.

Assembling the Banner

The first step in assembling the banner is to pin the design pieces into place. Place the paper pattern under the background fabric to guide you while pinning your

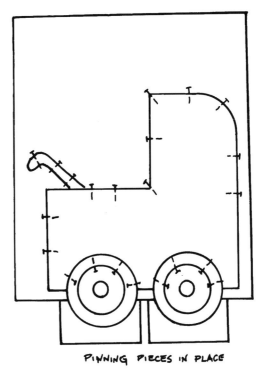

PINNING PIECES IN PLACE

Figure 9.7

pieces. First pin the tires and the carriage, making sure these pieces fit together properly. Also make sure the carriage is in the proper position so the marks on the edge of the tires are at the bottom edge of the banner. (See Fig. 9.7.) Now you can pin the carriage handle into place.

Take the banner to the ironing board and fuse the design pieces. Set your iron for high heat with steam. Remember to use a press cloth. Only the top half of the tires will be fused to the background, with the bottom half hanging off.

When these design pieces are all pinned and fused, you will need to pin one of the blankets into place. (Put one of the blanket pieces aside until later.) Pin it so the fusible

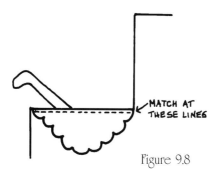

Figure 9.8

MATCH AT THESE LINES

thread stitching line on the blanket lines up exactly with the fused stitching line on the carriage. (See Fig. 9.8.) Then fuse the blanket into place. Notice that the blanket is fused at the top edge only.

Now that all the pieces are pinned and fused into place you can stabilize the fabric and start to appliqué. Sew around the handle first. To appliqué the carriage, start at the bottom where it meets one of the tires, and continue all the way around it, stitching across the blanket top and the carriage hood, until you meet the other tire. Then stop and then appliqué the small section of the carriage between the tires. (See Fig. 9.9.)

Now appliqué completely around the circumference of each tire. When you get to the area where the tire goes off the edge of the banner, simply satin stitch over the three lines of straight stitching as though you were appliquéing. To avoid having to stitch over the lower half of the tires again, you can shorten your stitch length here and make it very satiny. Remember you will be sewing on only one layer of fabric here. Don't forget to stabilize it.

Now that all design pieces are appliquéd into place, you can trim the background away behind the pieces. Pin the second blanket into place on the back of the banner in the same place as the first blanket. Fuse the edge of the blanket as before. Now you can appliqué the banner on the back. Catch the top edge of the blanket as you sew. Appliqué the carriage handle, carriage, and top half of the tire. Be sure to keep the blanket on the bottom side out of the way; otherwise you'll catch it in the satin stitching.

Add any accent stitching. From the front of the banner, using some sort of stabilizer, you can stitch the line separating the carriage hood from the carriage, and the spokes and hubs in the wheels, if you didn't do them earlier.

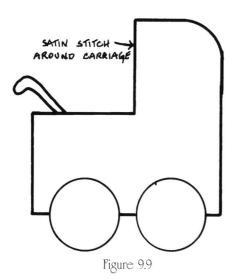

SATIN STITCH AROUND CARRIAGE

Figure 9.9

Sources of Supply

Clotilde, Inc.
2 Sew Smart Way
Stevens Point, WI 54481-8031
(800) 772-2891
   Threads, books, notions, sewing
      machine feet.
   Free Catalog

Kite Studio
555 Hamilton Blvd.
Wescosville, PA 18106
(610) 395-3560
   Complete line of banner-making
      supplies.
   Free Catalog

A Banner Year
P.O. Box 425
Elizabeth, PA 15037
(800) 720-2682
   Banner books; patterns for ban-
      ners, garden flags, and stained
      glass window banners; banner
      making supplies, banner hard-
      ware.
   Catalog $1.00

Nancy's Notions, Ltd.
33 Beichl Ave.
P.O. Box 683
Beaver Dam, WI 53916-0683
(800) 833-0690
   Threads, books, notions, sewing
      machine feet.
   Free Catalog

Speed Stitch
3113 Broadpoint Dr.
Harbor Heights, FL 33983
(800) 874-4119
   Decorative metallic, rayon, and
      invisible threads, machine em-
      broidery supplies, patterns,
      books, stabilizers.
   Catalog $3; refundable with order

Project Patterns

To enlarge any of the patterns on the pages that follow to the size called for in the directions, enlarge them on a copy machine until each grid square equals 1 inch. If you don't have access to a copy machine, see "Enlarging and Reducing Designs" on page 16.

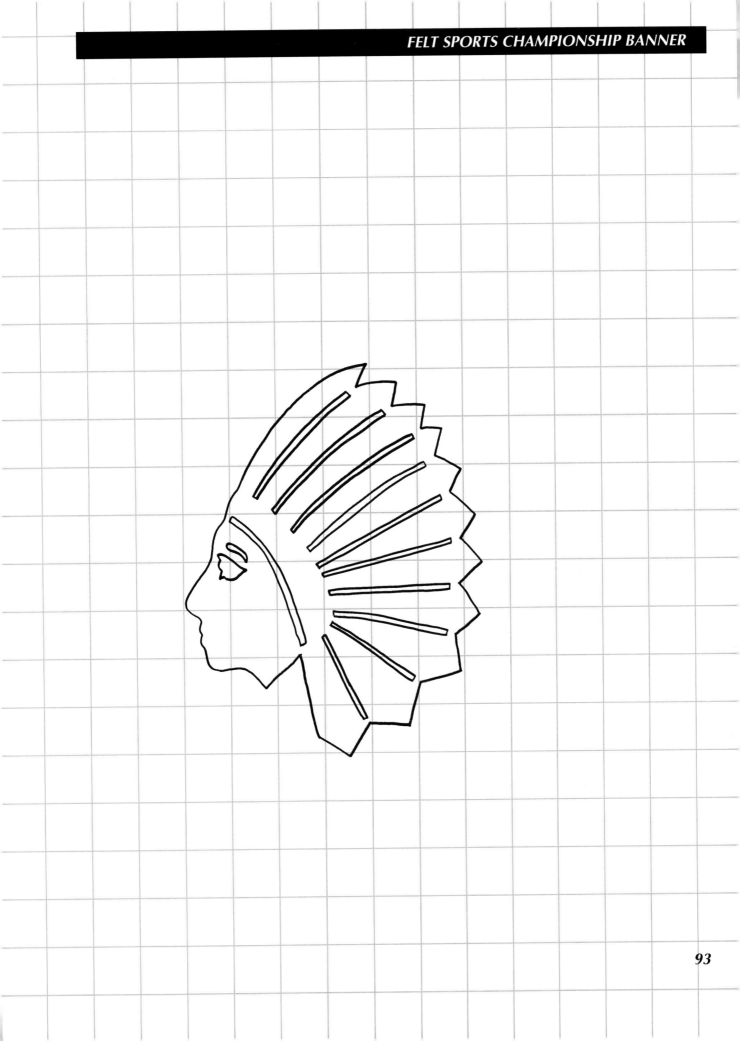

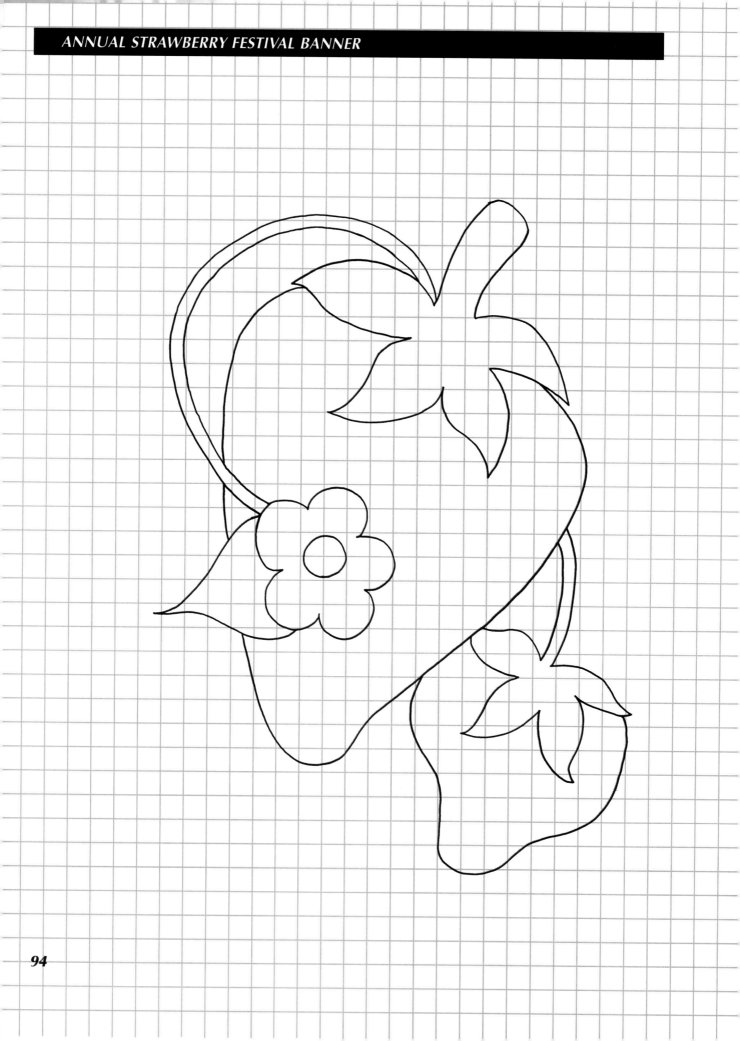

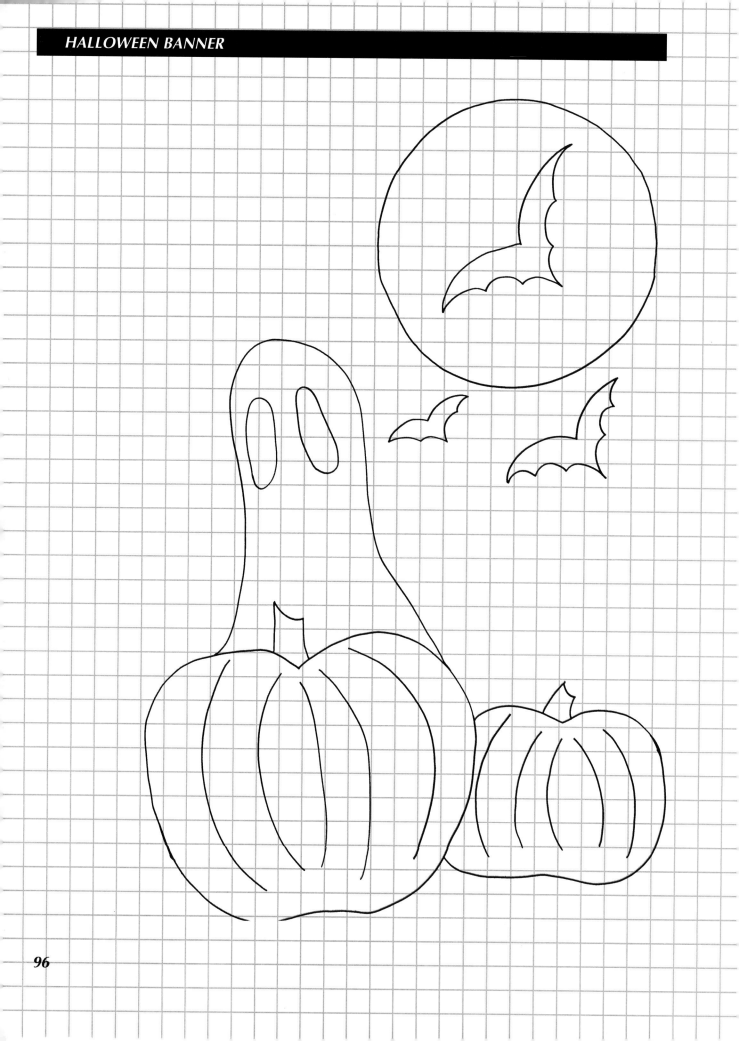

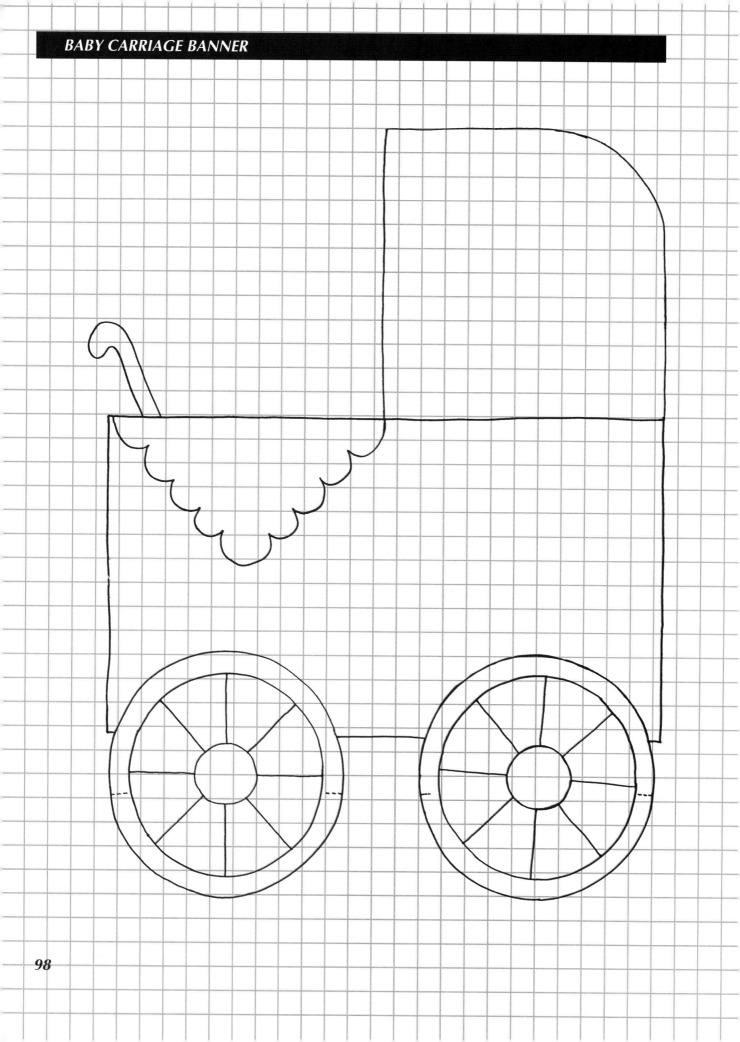

Index